I0816993

NEA PAPHOS
IV

ZAKŁAD ARCHEOLOGII ŚRÓDZIEMNOMORSKIEJ
POLSKIEJ AKADEMII NAUK
i
CENTRUM ARCHEOLOGII ŚRÓDZIEMNOMORSKIEJ
IM. KAZIMIERZA MICHAŁOWSKIEGO
UNIWERSYTETU WARSZAWSKIEGO

NEA PAPHOS
IV

Zofia Sztetyłło

STEMPLE CERAMICZNE
(1975—1989)

Warszawa 1991

CENTRE D'ARCHÉOLOGIE MÉDITERRANÉENNE
DE L'ACADÉMIE POLONAISE DES SCIENCES
et
CENTRE KAZIMIERZ MICHAŁOWSKI
D'ARCHÉOLOGIE MÉDITERRANÉENNE
DE L'UNIVERSITÉ DE VARSOVIE

NEA PAPHOS
IV

Zofia Sztetyłło
POTTERY STAMPS
(1975—1989)

Varsovie 1991

Traduction
IWONA ZYCH

Photographies
ZBIGNIEW DOLIŃSKI
WALDEMAR JERKE
JACEK M. KUCY
BOGDAN OKUPNY
TOMASZ SZMAGIER
ANDRZEJ WICHNIEWICZ
GRZEGORZ WYRZYKOWSKI

Couverture et jaquette du livre
MAŁGORZATA KARKOWSKA

Président du Comité de Rédaction
WIKTOR A. DASZEWSKI

Rédaction
JOLANTA MŁYNARCZYK
ADAM ŁAJTAR

ISBN 83-900096-6-8

Imprimé en Pologne
par la Maison
PHU sp. z o.o. „PARK"
BIELSKO-BIAŁA

CONTENTS

INTRODUCTION

Polish excavations in Nea Paphos cover a significant portion of the ancient city area — some twenty thousand square metres. They are located in the southwestern part of the ancient town, within the limits of the modern district of Malloutena. Investigations have resulted in the tracing of the original street network, which was based upon a regular orthogonal grid, and a determination of *insula* size. This layout, which originated in the Early Hellenistic period, apparently survived with little change into Late Roman times. Phases of habitation distinguished in this area begin in the late 4th century B.C. and continue down into the 6th century A.D. The various discovered architectural remnants, spanning almost a thousand years of the history of this site, include three larger and relatively well-preserved structures. Two of these date from the later Roman period: the so-called Villa of Theseus and the so-called House of Aion. The first is a large peristyle structure of the 2nd-4th centuries A.D., while the second was constructed in the 4th century A.D. and was presumably destroyed in the end of the same century. The third structure, the so-called Hellenistic House, located just south of the Villa of Theseus, originated most probably sometime in the 2nd century B.C. A structure of considerable size, it had a peristyle court surrounded by colonnaded porticoes and numerous rooms in the eastern and western wings. In view of its size, it should probably be considered a public building of some sort. An earthquake in the second half of the 1st century A.D. brought about its ultimate destruction.

Several other earlier structures were noted in various soundings made in the area of excavations. Overall, they belong to the Hellenistic and Early Roman period. The earliest of these were presumably simple habitations more often than not connected with some sort of workshop, mainly small metal foundries. In the later Hellenistic and Early Roman period their place was taken by larger complexes such as the Hellenistic House already mentioned and another large building displaying a high quality of mural and architectural decoration, found beneath the western wing of the Villa of Theseus. The latter structure was built probably in Early Roman times.

One of the frequent finds in buildings of all periods were stamped amphora handles, the most numerous group after pottery sherds, lamps and coins. Of course, the scientific value of these objects for the research conducted in this area is vastly different, depending on their state of preservation, but primarily on their archeological context. There are some that are well stratified, but the majority are surface finds. They are, nevertheless, interesting because, apart from having significance for statistical studies, they constitute indirect evidence of the relations of Nea Paphos with various parts of the ancient world. Of course, the picture provided of contacts, economic in this particular case, cannot be anything but fragmentary. Stamped amphora handles, although of doubtless importance as evidence of trade contacts, are not and should not be taken as sole testimony. Nor can they constitute evidence of the nature of these economic relations, the amphora being understood as a packing material or a container for a set amount of goods imported to Nea Paphos from abroad. Nor are stamped amphora handles determinative of cultural or political ties. There is evidence, provided by other objects, of firm relations with areas of the ancient world not represented or represented only marginally in the archeological material discussed in this study. A case in point are Paphian contacts with both Ptolemaic and Roman Egypt, Italy, Asia Minor and the Levantine coast. Therefore, it is clear that stamped amphora handles together with the wealth of information they carry, become valuable only in the wider context provided by all kinds of finds.

This study constitutes the next volume in the Nea Paphos archeological series which is devoted to a discussion of the results of the Polish excavations. Conclusions reached through an analysis of the available stamps, when confronted with results of other studies either published already or in preparation, will in the future enable a discussion of the development of the Hellenistic and Roman capital of Cyprus in its full complexity.

W.A. Daszewski
Warsaw 1989

POTTERY STAMPS FROM NEA PAPHOS 1975—1989

Ceramic stamps which are the object of this study come from excavations in Nea Paphos on Cyprus conducted by the Polish Archeological Mission directed by W.A. Daszewski. This volume covers the period from 1975 to 1989 (for earlier campaigns see Z. Sztetyłło, *Nea Paphos* I. *Les timbres céramiques* (*1965—1973*), Varsovie 1976).

The stamps were found either in one of three buildings excavated by the mission or in the immediate vicinity. The buildings comprise the so-called Villa of Theseus — a Roman villa residence, the adjacent so-called House of Aion decorated with fine mosaics and the so-called Late Hellenistic House which was destroyed in the 1st cent. A.D. by an earth tremor, whereupon the southern wing of the Villa of Theseus was constructed in its ruins. Most of the finds come from upper layers with disturbed stratigraphy; this concerns finds from earlier campaigns as well. Only a few could be specifically connected with any of the excavated complexes, e.g. stamps found in the Late Hellenistic House and a few recovered from sealed pottery deposits in the Villa of Theseus. The latter included objects from the test trench in the northern wing, which reached Hellenistic layers, and another test trench south of the southern wing. Finally, there were the infrequent stamps which were found in layers below the mosaic floors of the Villa of Theseus and the House of Aion.

The study comprises both the well preserved stamps presently stored in the Paphos Museum and the ones recorded solely for statistical purposes in an auxiliary register (IP). In the gathered material which consists of 255 objects, Rhodian stamps are definitely predominant, numbering 212 objects. Other centers are represented less numerously: Chios — 2 stamps, Group of Nikandros — 1 stamp, 5 stamps from Cos, 9 stamps from Cnidus. One object may be of Corinthian origin, five are uncertain.

Beside the majority of Greek stamps, there are 12 Latin ones, obviously representing the Roman period in Paphos. The 8 stamps preserved on so-called "mortaria" are dated similarly. Although it is too early to draw more extensive conclusions on the grounds of the material gathered so far, these stamps are just as important evidence of the economic life of the city as the Hellenistic stamps and have an informative value of undoubted significance in historical reasoning.

Rhodes

Of the 212 stamps from Rhodes 78 belong to eponyms, 80 to producers. Even were we to assume that more stamps of eponyms and producers should be found among the objects with damaged or obliterated surface, it would not change the more or less equal proportions between official stamps and workshop stamps. As far as chronology is concerned, the stamps, of both official and workshop variety, cover Grace's periods II to VI; missing are finds from the oldest period, but these are infrequent at other sites as well, owing to the sporadic character of stamping in period I. Stamps from period III (210—175 B.C.) predominate, but this should be considered rather an expression of the economic vitality of Rhodes at this time, than the specificity of Paphos itself. In all the chronological groups there are names that appear repeatedly, but the vast majority is represented once only.

From periods I—II there is one stamp of the eponym Nikon; the eponyms Eukles and Klearchos and the potter Epigonos are represented in period II stamps, while producers Aristeidas and Agoranax belong to the end of period II and beginning of period III. Overall, 6 names were recorded for the period before 210 B.C.; of these, the names of the eponym Klearchos and the producer Agoranax appeared twice.

The most numerous group of stamps from period III includes 25 names of eponyms and 16 names of producers. The eponyms are: Agemachos, Agestratos (2), Agloumbrotos, Athanodotos (2), Ainesidamos (5), Ainetor (2), Anaxiboulos (3), Aratophanes (3), Aristratos, Archidamos, Archilaidas, Archokrates, Damokles II (2), Dorchylidas, Thestor, Iasikrates, Kallikrates II (2), Kallikratidas II (8), Kleukrates, Kleonymos II (2), Kratidas, Nikasagoras II (2), Ksenophanes II (3), Pausanias II (2), Timasagoras and Philodamos (2).

The following names were recorded on the producers' stamps: Agathokles (2), Aineas, Amyntas, Antimachos, Aristarchos (4), Ariston (3), Aristion (3), Artemidoros, Damokrates I (3), Diodotos, Dios (2), Epikrates, Herakleitos, Iason (2), Hippokrates, Linos (2), Marsyas (5), Menekrates (2), Menodoros, Nanis, Olympos (3), Sokrates (3) and Timarchides and Philainios (2).

Belonging to period IV or to the turn of periods III and IV are stamps of the following eponyms: Aleximachos, Anaxandros, Archembrotos, Autokrates, Gorgon, Damainetos II, Heragoras, Xenophantos and Timourrodos — in all, ten names on eleven stamps. Among the names of producers recorded on 11 stamps there are: Aristokles, Anaxippidas, Imas (2), Mentor, Moschos, Midas (2), Nolos and Rhodon II (2).

The last two periods — V (146—108 B.C.) and VI (108—80 B.C.) — are meagerly represented, while the last period VII (80—30 B.C.) is not represented at all. From period V there are the names of 8 eponyms and 7 producers. The eponym list comprises: Aristanax, Aristodamos II, Aristombrotidas (2), Aristopolis, Archibios, Euanor, Hieron II (2), Teisamenos and Timotheos, Among the producers there are Agathon, Bromios, Glaukias, Damatrios, Eukleitos (4), Hieron and Timaratos. Period VI is represented by stamps of the eponyms Iason and Aristonomos and a stamp of the producer Mousaios.

Among the eponyms and producers listed above there are names which appear together on amphorae originating from other sites. It cannot be excluded that also among the Paphos stamps there are some which may have been combined together on particular amphorae, but unfortunately no relations of this sort have been preserved.

Additionally to the stamps of eponyms and producers, there are 52 stamps with obliterated surfaces, wholly or partially illegible. On some either titles or names of months have been preserved, thus adding to the number of eponymical stamps as well as to those of producers. Of the two stamps on lagynoi one seems to be Rhodian, while the other may have originated from Chios.

Other centres

Chios is represented by two stamps of Hikesios, who has been recorded previously on finds from Paphos. A stamp of Menophilos has been assigned to the Nikandros group, while Cos is considered the source of stamps on double-barrelled amphora handles, which are dated only generally to the Hellenistic period in view of the present state of research on this centre. The eight stamps from Cnidus include those of the *douviri* Aristainos and Eratidas, the eponym Theudotos, the eponym Hierokles (and Agathokles), and a fragmentarily preserved stamp with the name of Krates, a stamp quite probably from the *duoviri* group and four very damaged stamps.

Six stamps do not have a certain provenance. One of them may be Corinthian, another with the name of Archokrates may possibly be Rhodian from about 240 B.C., while the other four have no analogies which could facilitate identification.

The 12 Latin stamps are either Spanish or Italic, mostly from the first two centuries of our era. Just as the stamps on mortaria, they have analogies in material from other archaeological sites.

In the catalogue I have retained the order by provenance, distinguishing in the Rhodian material groups of stamps belonging to eponyms and to producers. With each group the order is alphabetical.

ABBREVIATIONS

Abbreviations of titles of periodicals according to *Archäologische Bibliographie*

Badal'janc = J.S. Badal'janc, "Novye chronologičeskie sootvetstvija ličnych imen na rodosskich amforach", *SovArch* 2, 1980, pp. 161—166

Benoit = F. Benoit, *L'épave du Grand Congloué à Marseille, Gallia* Suppl. XIV, Paris 1961

Bingen = J. Bingen, "Anses d'amphores de Crocodilopolis-Arsinoe", *ChrEg* 30, 1955, pp. 130—133

Bleckman 1907 = F. Bleckman, *De inscriptionibus quae leguntur in vasculis rhodiis*, Göttingen 1907

Bleckman 1912 = F. Bleckman, "Zu den rhodischen Eponymen Heliospriestern", *Klio* XII, 1912, pp. 249—258

Blinkenberg II = Ch. Blinkenberg, *Lindos, Fouilles de l'Acropole 1902—1904*, II, *Inscriptions*, Berlin-Copenhague 1941

Börker = C. Börker = "Griechische Amphorenstempel von Tell Half bis zum Persischen Golf", *BaM 7*, 1974, pp. 31—49

Breccia = E. Breccia, *Rapport sur la marche du Service du Musée pendant l'exercise 1919—1920*, Municipalité d'Alexandrie 1920

Brugnone = A. Brugnone, "Bolli anforari rodii della necropoli di Lilibeo. Altri bolli anforari della necropoli di Lilibeo", ΚΩΚΑΛΟΣ. *Studi publicati dall'Istituto di storia antica dell'Università di Palermo* XXXII, 1968, pp. 19—113

Callender = M.H.C. Callender, *Roman Amphorae with Index of Stamps*, London 1965

Calvet 1972 = Y. Calvet, *Salamine de Chypre*, III, *Les timbres amphoriques* (*1965—1970*), Paris 1972

Calvet 1978 = Y. Calvet, "Timbres amphoriques de Salamine 1971—1974", *RDAC* 1978, pp. 222—231

Calvet 1982 = Y. Calvet, *Kition-Bamboula*, I, *Les timbres amphoriques*, Paris 1982

Canarache = V. Canarache, *Importul amforelor stampilate la Istria*, Bucureşti 1967

Criscuolo = L. Criscuolo, *Bolli d'anfore greci e romani. La collezione dell'Università Cattolica di Milano*, (= *Studi di Storia Antica* 6), Bologna 1982

Crowfoot = J.W. Crowfoot, "Potter's Stamps", *Samaria — Sebaste*, III, *The Objects from Samaria*, London 1957, pp. 379—388

Dunand = M. Dunand, *Fouilles de Byblos*, I, (*1926—1932*), Paris 1939

Empereur = J.—Y. Empereur, "Timbres amphoriques de Crocodilopolis-Arsinoé", *BIFAO 77*, 1977, pp. 197—233

Gaertringen, Rhodos = F. Hiller von Gaertringen, "Rhodos", *Paulys Realenzyclopedie der Klassischen Altertumswissenschaft*, Supplementband V, 1931, cols. 834—840

Gentili = C.V. Gentili, "I timbri anforari rodii nel Museo Nazionale di Siracusa", *Archivio Storico Siracusano* IV, 1, 1958, pp. 18—95

Grace 1934 = V. Grace, "Stamped Amphorae Handles found in 1931—1932", *Hesperia* III, 1934, pp. 197—310

Grace 1948 = V. Grace, "Rhodian Jars in Florida", *Hesperia* XVII, 1948, pp. 144—147

Grace 1949 = V. Grace, "Standard Pottery Containers of the Ancient Greek World", *Hesperia*, Suppl. VIII, 1949, pp. 175—189

Grace 1950 = V. Grace, "Stamped Amphorae Handles", *Tarsus*, I, *Excavations at Gözlü Kule*, Princeton 1950, pp. 175—189

Grace 1952 = V. Grace, "Timbres amphoriques trouvés à Delos", *BCH* 76, 1952, pp. 514—540

Grace 1953 = V. Grace, "The Eponyms named on Rhodian Amphora Stamps", *Hesperia*, XXII, 1953, pp. 116—128

Grace 1956 = V. Grace, "Stamped Wine Jar Fragments", *Hesperia*, Suppl. X, *Small Objects from the Pnyx*, 1956, pp. 113—198

Grace, Canaanite = V. Grace, "The Canaanite Jar", *The Aegean in the Near East, Studies Presented to Hetty Goldmann*, Locust Valley 1956, pp. 80—109

Grace, Amphoras = V. Grace, *Amphoras and the Ancient Wine Trade, Excavations of the Athenian Agora, Picture Book no, 6,* Princeton 1961

Grace 1962 = V. Grace, "Stamped Amphora Handles of Commercial Amphoras", *Excavations at Nessana*, I, London 1962, pp. 106—130

Grace 1963 = V. Grace, "Notes on the Amphoras from the Koroni Peninsula", *Hesperia* XXXII, 1963, pp. 319—334

Grace 1965 = V. Grace "The Commercial Amphoras from the Antikythera Shipwreck", *Transactions of the American Philosophical Society* 55, 1965, pp. 5—17

Grace 1968 = V. Grace, "Die gestampelten Amphorenhenkel aus stratigraphisch gesicherten Fundzusammenhängen", *Altertümer von Pergamon*, XI, 1, *Das Asklepieion*, Berlin 1968, pp. 175—179

Grace-Savvatianou = V. Grace, M. Savvatianou-Petropoulakou, "Les timbres amphoriques grecs", *Exploration archéologique de Délos*, XXVII, *L'ilot de la Maison des Comédiens*, Paris 1970, pp. 277—382

Grace 1974 = V. Grace, "Revisions in Early Hellenistic Chronology", *AM* 89, 1974, pp. 193—200

Grace, Kyme I = V. Grace, "Stamped Amphora Handles", *Kyme*, I, *Anatolian Collection of Charles University*, Praha 1974, pp. 89—98

Grace 1985 = V. Grace, "The Middle Stoa dated by Amphora Stamps", *Hesperia* LIV, 1985, pp. 1—54

Grace 1986 = V. Grace, "Some Amphoras from a Hellenistic Wreck", *BCH*, Suppl. XIII, 1986, pp. 551—565

Gramatopol-Poenaru Bordea, Tomis = M. Gramatopol, Ch. Poenaru-Bordea, "Amfore stampilate din Tomis", *Studi şi Cercetari de Istorie Veche* XIX, 1, 1968, pp. 41—61

Gramatopol-Poenaru Bordea, Dacia XIII = M. Gramatopol, Ch. Poenaru-Bordea, "Amphora Stamps from Callatis and South Dobrudja", *Dacia* XIII, 1969, pp. 127—282

Hall = I.H. Hall, "The Greek Stamps of the Handles of Rhodian Amphoras found in

Cyprus and now in the Metropolitan Museum of New York", *JAOS* XI, 1885, pp. 390—395
Hayes = J.W. Hayes, "North Syrian Mortaria", *Hesperia* XXXVI, 4, 1967, pp. 337—347
Kent = J.H. Kent, "Stamped Amphora Handles from the Delian Temple Estates", *Studies presented to David Moore Robinson*, II, Washington University, St. Louis 1953, pp. 127—134
Lazarov 1974 = M. Lazarov, "Amfornite pečati ot Odessos", *BullVarna* X(XXV), pp. 19—54
Lazarov 1977 = M. Lazarov, "Trgovskite bržki na Rodos s zapadnopontijskite gradove prez elenističeskata epocha", *BullVarna* XIII(XXVIII), 1977, pp. 1—47
Lenger 1955 = M.T. Lenger, "Timbres amphoriques trouvés à Argos", *BCH* LXXIX, 1955, pp. 484—508
Lenger 1957 = M.T. Lenger, "Timbres amphoriques trouvés à Argos (Deuxième serie), *BCH* LXXXI, 1957, pp. 160—180
Levi 1964 = E.I. Levi, "Keramičeskij kompleks III-II v. do n.e. iz raskopok ol'vijskoj Agory", *Ol'via, Temenos i Agora*, Moskva 1964, pp. 225—280
Levi, Festos = D. Levi, "Bolli d'anfore e pesi fittili da Festos", *ASAtene* 43—44, 1965—1966, pp. 574—577
Levi, Iasos = D. Levi, "Nuovi bolli vascolari da Iasos", *ASAtene* 43—44, 1965—1966, pp. 547—567
Levi-Pugliese Caratelli = D. Levi, C. Pugliese Caratelli, "Nuove iscrizioni di Iasos", *ASAtene* 39—40, 1961—1962, pp. 605—629
Macalister = R.A. Macalister, *The Excavations at Gezer*, II, London 1912
Maiuri = A. Maiuri, "Una fabrica di anfore rodie", *ASAtene* IV—V, 1921—1922, pp. 249—269
Meyet 1978 = F. Meyet, "Marques d'amphore de Mauretanie Tingitaine", *MEFRA* XC, 1, 1978, pp. 357—406
Mertens = J. Mertens, "Marques d'amphores. Les fouilles d'Alba Fucens", *AntCl* XXIV, 1955, pp. 51—93
Mirčev = M. Mirčev, *Amfornite pečati ot Muzeia v Varna*, Sofia 1958
Nachtergael = G. Nachtergael, *La collection Marcel Hombert*, I, *Timbres amphoriques et autres documents écrits acquis en Égypte*, (= *Papyrologica Bruxellensia* 115), Bruxelles 1978
Nicolaou-Empereur = I. Nicolaou, J.-Y. Empereur, "Amphores rhodiennes du Musée de Nicosie", *BCH*, Suppl. XIII, 1986, pp. 513—531
Nilsson = M.P. Nilsson, "Timbres amphoriques de Lindos publiés avec une étude sur les timbres amphoriques rhodiens", *Bulletin de l'Academie Royale des Sciences et des Lettres de Danemark*, Copenhague 1909, pp. 37—180, 349—539
Paris = J. Paris, "Une nouvelle collection rhodienne de timbres amphoriques", *Mélanges Holleaux*, Paris 1913, pp. 153—175
Paris 1914 = J. Paris, "Timbres amphoriques de Rhodes", *BCH* XXXVIII, 1914, pp. 300—326
Pellegrini = A. Pellegrini, "Iscrizioni ceramiche d'Erice e sui dintorni", *Archivio Storico Siciliano* XII, 1887, pp. 184—303
Porro = G.G. Porro, "Bolli d'anfore rodie trovati in Sardegna", *Archivio Storico Sardo* X, 1914, pp. 380—389
Porro 1916 = G.G. Porro, "Bolli d'anfore del Museo Nazionale Romano", *ASAtene* II, 1916, pp. 103—124

Pridik = E.M. Pridik, *Inventarnyj katalog klejm na amfornych ručkach i gorlyškach i na čerepiščach Ermitažnogo sobranija,* Petrograd 1917
Pridik 1926 = E.M. Pridik, "Zu den rhodischen Amphorenstempeln", *Klio* XX, 1926, pp. 303—331
Reisner = C.A. Reisner, *Harvard Excavations at Samaria, 1908—1910,* Cambridge 1924
Le Roy = Chr. Le Roy, "Timbres amphoriques provenat de Tanis", *BCH* XCIX, 1975, pp. 235—246
Le Roy, BIFAO 84 = Chr. LeRoy, Timbres amphoriques provenant de Tanis: complement", *BIFAO* 84, 1984, pp. 307—316
Säflund = M.L. Säflund, *Stamped Amphora Handles. Labraunda, Swedish Excavations and Researches,* II, 2, Stockholm 1980
Schuchhardt = C. Schuchhardt, "Die Inschriften von Pergamon", *Altertümer von Pergamon* VIII, 2, Berlin 1985, pp. 423—499
Šelov 1956 = D.B. Šelov, "Keramičeskie klejma iz raskopok Fanagorii", *MIA* 57, 1956, pp. 128—153
Šelov 1957 = D.B. Sělov, "Klejma na amforach i čerepiščach najdennych pri raskopkach Pantikapeja v 1945—1949 g.", *MIA* 56 1957, pp. 202—226
Šelov 1966 = D.B. Šelov, "Dopolnitel'nye klejma radosskich amfor", *Mélanges offerts à K. Michałowski,* Varsovie 1966, pp. 663—668
Šelov 1975 = D.B. Šelov, *Keramičeskie klejma iz raskopok Tanaisa III—I vekov do n.e.,* Moskva 1975
Štearman = E.M. Štearman, "Keramičeskie klejma iz Tiry", *KSIIMK* XXXVI, 1951, pp. 31—49
Sztetyłło 1963 = Z. Sztetyłło, "Stamped Amphora Handles from Polish Exavations in Tell Atrib (1957—1961), *Eos* LIII, 2, 1963, pp. 335—340
Sztetyłło 1975 = Z. Sztetyłło, "Timbres amphoriques grecs des fouilles polonaises à Alexandrie (1962—1972)", *EtTrav* VIII, 1975, pp. 159—235
Sztetyłło 1976 = Z. Sztetyłło, *Les timbres céramiques (1965—1973). Nea Paphos,* I, Varsovie 1976
Sztetyłło 1978 = Z. Sztetyłło, "Timbres céramiques des fouilles polonaises à Alexandrie (1973—1974)", *EtTrav* X, 1978, pp. 259—616
Sztetyłło 1983 = Z. Sztetyłło, *Les timbres céramiques dans les collections du Musée National de Varsovie,* Varsovie 1983
Sztetyłło 1984 = Z. Sztetyłło, "Timbres céramiques des fouilles polonaises à Nea Paphos en 1978", *EtTrav* XIII, 1984, pp. 366—370
Sztetyłło RDAC 1984 = Z. Sztetyłło, "Les timbres amphoriques", [in:] "Fouilles polonaises à Kato Paphos, Chantier de Maloutena", *RDAC* 1984, pp. 311—314, pl. LXX
Sztetyłło = Z. Sztetyłło, "Les timbres céramiques des fouilles polonaises à Alexandrie (1974—1979)", *EtTrav* XIV, 1990, pp. 160—212

CATALOGUE

RHODES

Eponyms

1. Inv. no. WS 5/1982
Villa of Theseus, southern wing, upper layer
Diam.: 3.5 cm
Circular stamp with a representation of a rose in the centre surrounded by the legend:
'Επὶ 'Αγεμάχ[ου Σμι]νϑίου

The activity of this eponym should be dated to period III owing to the presence of his stamps in the assemblage discovered at Pergamon[1]. An analysis of the Rhodian stamps from Sinope, among which the name of Agemachos was to be found, led Robinson[2] to connect the whole group to a transport of 10 000 amphorae from Rhodes to Sinope in 220 B.C., referred to by Polybius. Other proposals for a closer dating of this eponym's activity were made on the grounds of the coincidence of his name with that of Agemachos occurring on Rhodian coins of the 3rd—2nd cent. B.C.[3], the name of Agemachos Gorgonos who held the office of *hierothytas* in Lindos in 240 B.C.[4], or finally the name of Agemachos who was the priest of Athena Lindia in 135 B.C.[5]

Further possibilities for narrowing down the dating of this eponym are created by an analysis of the names of Rhodian producers who stamped the same amphorae as Agemachos. One of these is Ariston[6] and another Damokrates I who, according to V. Grace, was the first to use small subsidiary stamps around 188 B.C.[7] The concurrence on the same amphora of the stamps of these producers with those of other known Rhodian eponyms places Agemachos' activity in the period 210—175 B.C..

Stamps of Agemachos are frequently encountered on various archaeological sites[8].

[1] Schuchhardt, nos. 775—793; Grace 1952, p. 528.
[2] Robinson, *AJA* 1905, pp. 296—297; Polyb. IV, 56.
[3] Nachtergael, p. 37 no. 11; BMC Caria, p. 242, 129.
[4] Blinkenberg II, 1, 132 no. 103 11.
[5] Blinkenberg II, 1, 23, 507 no. 225 b.
[6] Bleckmann 1907, p. 31; Bleckmann 1912, p. 252; Badal'janc, p. 164.
[7] Paris 1914, p. 122; Badal'janc, p. 164. Damokrates I cf. Grace 1968, p. 175 nos. 2—3; Grace-Savvatianou, pp. 291 and 295 note 1, 371, 380; Grace 1985, p. 8; Šelov 1956, p. 137, 140, nos. 17, 18, 76.
[8] Gaertringen, Rhodos, 835 no. 2; Nilsson, no. 8; Paris 1914, p. 301 II; Porro 1916, p. 109 no. 3; Grace 1952, p. 528; Kent, p. 132 no. 9; Calvet 1972 no. 46; Calvet 1982, p. 16; Sztetyłło 1976 no. 23; Pridik, p. 1 nos. 1—5; Levi 1964, nos. 1—2; Šelov 1975, no. 1; Sztetyłło 1959, no. 424; Sztetyłło 1983, no. 15; Lazarov 1977, p. 22 no. 1; Mirčev, nos. 81—82; Gramatopol-Poenaru Bordea, Dacia XIII, no. 696; Gramatopol-Poenaru Bordea, Tomis, p. 55 no. 33; Nachtergael, no. 11; Sztetyłło 1975, p. 172 nos. 37—38; Reisner, p. 314; Crowfoot, p. 380; Dunand, p. 17; Börker, p. 39 no. 17; Gentili, p. 39 no. 26; Brugnone, p. 5 no. 1.

2. Inv. no. 3/1985
Villa of Theseus, western wing, sector 1/85, layer 1
Dimensions: 3 × 5 cm
Rectangular stamp with the legend in three lines:
’Επὶ ’Αγε-
στράτου
Δαλίου

Agestratos himself is not recorded among the eponyms known from Pergamon finds, his stamps concur with those of the producer Agathokles II who did appear in the Pergamon group; both should therefore be placed in period III[9]. The producer's dating is further corroborated by the appearance of his name together with the names of other eponyms of this period[10]. More exactly, according to Grace, the activity of Agestratos II, to whom this stamp belongs, should be placed around 182 B.C.[11]

Stamps of Agestratos have been recorded in Rhodes, Delos, Cyprus, on the coast of the Black Sea, in areas of the ancient Near East and elsewhere[12].

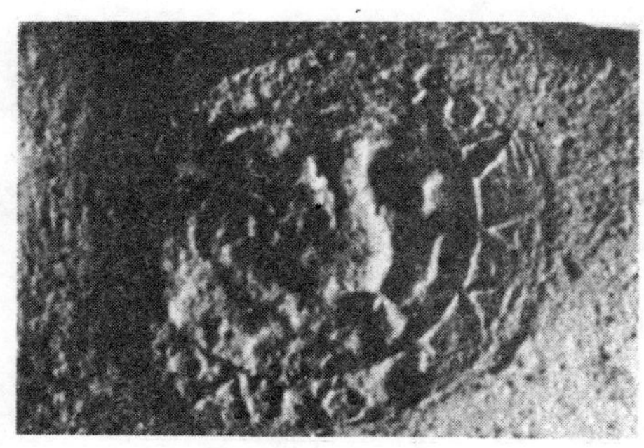

3. Inv. no. 24/1986
House of Aion, room 3, above the debris of a wall
Diam.: 3 cm
Circular stamp with a representation of a rose and encircling legend:
[’Επὶ ’Αγεστ]ράτου Δαλίου rose
Tentatively reconstructed as a stamp of the eponym Agestratos. See no. 2 above.

[9] Schuchhardt, nos. 766—774; see also Bleckmann 1907, p. 22 and 31; Porro, p. 385 no. 43; Gentili, p. 27 and 29; Badal'janc, p. 163; Grace 1952, p. 528; Grace-Savvatianou, no. E 45; Lazarov 1977, p. 21 no. 1;

[10] One should mention such eponyms as, for example, Symmachos, see Gentili, p. 37, no. 20a—b; Athanodotos, see Grace 1949, p. 180, no. 23. One other combination of Agestratos II with Philainios is known, see Badal'janc, p. 165.

[11] Grace 1985, p. 8.

[12] Nilsson, p. 353, no. 9; Grace 1952, p. 528; Grace-Savvatianou, p. 301, no. E 45; Sztetyłło 1976, p. 32, nos. 25—26; Levi 1964, nos. 3—9; Lazarov 1974, p. 48, no. 46; Lazarov 1977, p. 22, no. 3; Sztetyłło 1975, no. 39; Sztetyłło 1978, no. 14; Sztetyłło 1990, nos. 2—3; Börker, p. 38, no. 14; Crowfoot, p. 380; Gentili, p. 36, no. 16.

4. Inv. no. 28/1986
Villa of Theseus, southern wing, within the hypocaustum
Dimensions: 4.5 × 3 cm
Rectangular stamp with the legend in two lines:
'Επὶ 'Αγ [λουμ-]
βρότου
The name of the eponym Agloumbrotos was recorded among the Pergamon stamp finds[13]. This permitted Grace to place him in the period between 210 and 175 B.C.[14] and then narrow this down further to 188—175 B.C.[15] Stamps with the name of the eponym Agloumbrotos are encountered on many archaeological sites[16].

5. Inv. no. 31/1978
Villa of Theseus, northern wing, upper layer
Diam.: 3 cm
Legend: 'Επὶ 'Αϑανοδότου ['Υα]κινϑίου rose
In conformity with the data supplied by the Pergamon finds[17], Grace dates this eponym to the period 188—183 B.C.[18] He cooperated with the following producers: Damokrates[19], and Hippokrates[20] as well as Agathokles[21], Amyntas[22], Antimachos[23], Ariston[24], Sarapion[25], Philainios[26]. Various stamps of Athanodotos are encountered on many archaeological sites[27].

[13] Schuchhardt, no. 805. See also Bleckmann 1912, p. 252, no. 11; Gaertringen, Rhodos, no. 13.
[14] Grace 1952, p. 528.
[15] Grace 1985, p. 8; Grace 1953, p. 121 note 13.
[16] Nilsson, no. 17; Paris 1914, pp. 301—302, IV; Porro 1916, p. 109, no. 2; Grace 1952, p. 528; Pridik, p. 2, nos 14—18; Šelov 1975, nos. 3—4; Empereur 1977, no. 5; Reisner, p. 313; Macalister, p. 352; Crowfoot, p. 380; Porro, p. 383, no. 23; Pellegrini, p. 198, no. 15; Brugnone, p. 6, no. 2.
[17] Schuchhardt, nos. 809—819.
[18] Grace 1952, p. 528; Grace 1985, pp. 8—10.
[19] Grace 1985, p. 10.
[20] Grace 1985, p. 10, and Grace, Kyme 1, p. 94, A 3.
[21] Grace 1949, no. 23; Grace 1985, p. 10.
[22] Nicolaou-Empereur, no. 3; Grace 1985, p. 10.
[23] Badal'janc, p. 164; Grace 1985, p. 10.
[24] Grace 1985, p. 10.
[25] Loc. cit.
[26] Loc. cit.
[27] Nilsson, no. 25; Paris, p. 302, VI; Porro 1916, no. 9; Grace 1950, no. 29; Calvet 1972, no. 47; Sztetyłło 1976, no. 46; Sztetyłło 1984, nos. 1—3; Calvet 1978, nos. 5—6; Pridik, nos. 19—24; Šelov 1975, nos. 6—8; Levi 1964, nos. 11—32; Breccia, p. 21;Sztetyłło 1975, no. 61; Sztetyłło 1978, no. 17; Crowfoot, p. 380; Reisner, p. 314; Brugnone, no. 111.

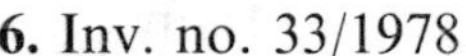

6. Inv. no. 33/1978
Villa of Theseus, northern wing
Diam.: 3 cm
Legend: ’Επὶ ’Αθανοδ[ότου   rose
A stamp of the eponym Athanodotos: see no. 5.

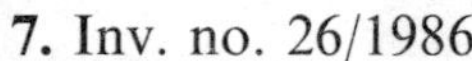

7. Inv. no. 26/1986
House of Aion, room 3, sector 2, layer 1
Dimensions: 3.2 × 1 cm
Narrow elongated rectangle with a two-line inscription. Lunate *sigma.*
’Επὶ Αἰνησιδάμου
Θεσμοφορίου

Of the two Rhodian eponyms of this name the activity of Ainesidamos I falls in period I, i.e. end of the 4th — beginning of the 3rd cent. B.C., while Ainesidamos II is dated to period III, that is 210—175 B.C.[28] Our stamp seems to belong to the second one of these two. Stamps of this eponym were found in Pergamon[29] and he appears together with such producers of period III as Olympos[30] and Sokrates[31], whose names repeatedly appear on amphorae stamped by other eponyms of this period[32].

Stamps with the name Ainesidamos have been recorded in Rhodes, Delos, Cyprus, areas of the ancient Near East and in other regions[33].

8. Inv. no. 34/1987
House of Aion, northwest of the foundations of room 1
Dimensions: 3.5 × 1.3 cm
Narrow elongated rectangle with two lines of legend:
’Επὶ Αἰνησιδάμ(ου)
Θεσμοφορίου
See above no. 7.

[28] Grace 1952, p. 528; Grace 1953,p. 122, no. 14; Grace 1963, p. 328 note 1.
[29] Schuchhardt, nos. 829—840. See also Gaertringen, Rhodos, 835, no. 22.
[30] Pridik 1926, p. 329 and 331; Badal’janc, p. 165.
[31] Grace 1949, p. 180, no. 21; Grace-Savvatianou, p. 279 note 2.
[32] The name of Sokrates is known from amphorae stamped with the names of the following eponyms, all of period III: Xenophanes II, Hieron I, Sodamos, Sostratos, Archidamos and Symmachos. See Grace-Savvatianou, p. 303, nos E 3 and E 5, and p. 279 note 2, p. 296 note 1, and p. 371. Also Grace, Kyme 1, p. 95; Schuchhardt, p. 426; Bleckmann 1907, p. 22 and 31; Badal’janc, p. 165.
[33] Nilsson, no. 30; Grace 1952, p. 528; Sztetyłło 1976, nos. 27—31; Sztetyłło 1984, p. 367, no. 3; Pridik, p. 3, no. 27; Levi 1964, nos. 40—47; Šelov 1975, no. 9; Lazarov 1974, pp. 48—49; Lazarov 1977, p. 22, no. 9; Mirčev, nos. 84—85; Sztetyłło 1983, no. 136; Canarache, no. 508; Nachtergael, p. 37, no. 12; Breccia, p. 21, no. 11; Gentili, no. 35; Empereur 1977, p. 205, no. 11; Crowfoot, p. 380.

9. Inv. no. 10/1977
Surface find
Dimensions: 3.6 × 1.4 cm

'Επὶ Αἰν[ησιδ]άμ(ου)
Θεσμο[φορ]ίου

The first letters of a two-line stamp of the eponym Ainesidamos II containing also the name of the month Thesmophorios. See no. 7 above.

10. Inv. no. 30/1978
Villa of Theseus, northern wing, upper layer
Diam.: 3 cm

['Επὶ Αἰνησιδ]άμου 'Αρταμιτ[ίου]   rose

The preserved ending of the name suggests that the stamp may have been that of Ainesidamos II; the month is Artamitios.

11. Inv. no. IP 1980
In the vicinity of the Villa of Theseus
Dimensions: 3.5 × 1.5 cm

'Ε[πὶ Α]ἰν[ησι-]
δά[μου]
Δαλίου

Stamp of the eponym Ainesidamos II. See no. 7 above.

12. Inv. no. 11/1983
Villa of Theseus, northern wing, sector 3/83, upper layer
Diam: 3 cm

Circular stamp with a representation of a rose in the centre and encircling inscription:

'Επὶ Αἰνήτορος Πανάμου   rose

The presence of stamps with the name of the eponym Ainetor in Pergamon placed this eponym in period III[34]. The date of this official could be determined more closely owing to the concurrence of his stamps with those of the producer Aristarchos[35]. The latter had cooperated in the years 188—183 B.C. with other eponyms of period III[36] and it is to these years that his work with Ainetor dates.

Stamps of Ainetor were found on Rhodes, Cyprus, Delos, the Black Sea coast, regions of the ancient Near East and elsewhere[37].

[34] Schuchhardt, nos. 841—853; Grace 1952, p. 528.
[35] Such a combination appears on an amphora from Monte Iudica. See Brugnone, p. 7, no. 3 note 30.
[36] Symmachos was one of these eponyms, see Gentili, p. 35, nos. 9—10. Grace attributes Symmachos to this period, see Grace-Savvatianou, p. 291 and 295 note 1, and p. 371. Symmachos was one of the first eponyms who

13. Inv. no. IP 8/1982
Villa of Theseus, northern wing, upper layer
Dimensions: 4.3 × 1.5 cm
Rectangular stamp with three lines of legend. Surface damaged extensively making the reconstruction highly tentative.
'Επὶ Αἰνήτο-
ρος
Δαλίου

Assuming the reading is correct, the stamp belonged to the eponym Ainetor. See no. 12 above.

14. Inv. no. 20/1979
Villa of Theseus, room 69, layer 5 in well
Dimensions: 4.2 × 1.8 cm
['Επὶ 'Αλε]ξι-
μάχου
Καρνείου

The activity of the eponym Aleximachos falls between the years 175—146 B.C.[38]; he cooperated with such producers of the period as Andrikos[39], Antimachos[40], Eukleitos[41], Hermias[42], Manes[43] and Menothemis[44], who are dated by the stamps of other eponyms of the period concurring with them.

Small subsidiary stamps are also encountered with the stamps of Aleximachos[45].

Stamps of this eponym are found on many Mediterranean sites as well as on the Black Sea coast and in regions of the ancient Near East[46].

15. Inv. no. IP 9/1982
Villa of Theseus, northern wing, sector 9/82, upper layer
Dimensions: 4 × 1.7 cm
Rectangular stamp with a three-line inscription:
'Επὶ 'Αναξάν-
δρου
Δαλίου

The name of the eponym Anaxandros has not been recorded either among the stamps from Per-

introduced the custom of using small subsidiary stamps beside the large ones, this as a result of his cooperation with the producer Damokrates I, see Grace 1985, p. 45, no. 1, and Grace 1968, p. 175, no. 3 — the combination Symmachos — Damokrates. See also Badal'janc, p. 164.

37 Nilsson, no. 31; Maiuri, p. 262; Grace 1952, p. 528; I. Nicolaou, *RDAC* 1965, p. 115, 4 b; Pridik, p. 3, nos. 28—37 and p. 132, nos. 10—11; Levi 1964, p. 262, no. 48; Lazarov 1977, p. 23, no. 10; Sztetyłło 1983, p. 33, no. 32; Reisner, p. 313; Macalister, p. 353; Crowfoot, p. 380; Breccia, p. 22, no. 12; Pellegrini, p. 204, nos. 63—70; Gentili, p. 42, no. 36; Brugnone, p. 7, nos. 3—4.

38 Grace 1950, p. 136 and 142, nos. 39—40; Grace, Kyme 1, p. 94, A 5.

39 Grace, Kyme 1, p. 96, A 5.

40 Pridik 1926, pp. 309, 321, 331; Badal'janc, p. 163.

41 Badal'janc, p. 164.

42 Loc. cit.

43 Loc. cit.

44 Grace, Kyme 1, p. 94.

45 A small rose flower is also typical of Hippokrates. See Grace, Kyme 1, p. 94.

46 Nilsson, no. 39; Grace 1952, p. 528; Grace 1950, pp. 136, 142, nos. 39—40; Grace 1934, no. 20; Pridik, nos. 47—49; Šelov 1975, no. 17; Sztetyłło 1976, nos. 139—140; Empereur 1977, no. 12; Sztetyłło 1975, no. 17; Sztetyłło 1990, nos. 35—37; Crowfoot, p. 380; Börker, no. 26; Reisner, p. 314; Macalister, p. 353; Brugnone, no. 6; Sztetyłło 1983, no. 58.

gamon or in other well dated archeological assemblages. In Grace's opinion, he should be placed about the second half of the 2nd cent B.C.[47]

Stamps with the name of this eponym are rare[48].

16. Inv. no. 36/1986
Villa of Theseus, western wing, surface find
Dimensions: 4.5 × 1.8 cm
Rectangular stamp with an inscription in two lines:
'Επὶ 'Αναξιβούλου
Σμινθίου

Stamps with the name of the eponym Anaxiboulos were found in the Pergamon assemblage and on this basis his activity was dated to the end of period III[49]. He is found together with such producers as Nysios[50]; since Nysios worked also with eponyms of period IV, i.e. Aratophanes I and Pausanias III[51], Anaxiboulos may perhaps be dated to a little later, after 175 B.C. Of course, it is possible that Nysios himself worked in the end of period III and the beginning of period IV and that Anaxiboulos was eponym at this time as well, primarily in the last years of period III (before 175 B.C.).

Stamps of Anaxiboulos are among the more frequent stamps encountered on many archaeological sites[52].

17. Inv. no. 9/1989
Late Hellenistic House, stone fill ca 0,9—1 m down from the surface
Dimensions: 3.5 × 1.3 cm
'Επὶ 'Αναξι-
βούλου
Θεσμοφορίου

Stamps of the eponym Anaxiboulos, month Thesmophorios. See no. 16 above.

[47] Grace 1952, p. 528; Nicolaou-Empereur, pp. 525—526, no. 10 (a combination with the producer Hieron). The authors inform that Anaxandros' stamps are dated also by amphorae stamped by the producer Andronikos, in view of the concurrence of their stamps. Andronikos himself is dated reliably to this period by a concurrence of his stamps with the marks of the eponyms Aleximachos and Xenophantos.

[48] See above and also Nilsson, no. 46; Grace 1934, p. 230, no. 58; Grace 1953, p. 122, no. 22; Le Roy, p. 236, no. 2; Le Roy, BIFAO 84, p. 308, no. 1; Breccia, pp. 22—23, no. 19; Gramatopol-Poenaru Bordea, Dacia XIII, no. 702; Gramatopol-Poenaru Bordea, Tomis, no. 25; Pridik, p. 4, no. 52; Šelov 1975, nos. 18—19; Lazarov 1977, p. 23, no. 15.

[49] Schuchhardt, no. 860; Grace 1952, p. 528; Grace-Savvatianou, p. 291 note 2. See also Gaertringen, Rhodos, 835, no. 35, and Grace 1953, p. 122, no. 62.

[50] Porro, p. 385, nos. 47—48; Badal'janc, p. 165.

[51] For the combination: Aratophanes — Nysios see Porro, p. 381, nos. 3—4; For the combination: Pausanias III — Nysios see Grace-Savvatianou, no. E 12.

[52] Nilsson, no. 47; Paris 1914, p. 303, IX; Porro 1916, p. 109, no. 15; Grace 1952, p. 528; Calvet 1982, no. 22; Sztetyłło 1976, nos. 43—44; Sztetyłło 1975, p. 174, nos. 42—43; Sztetyłło 1990, nos. 14—16; Empereur 1977, p. 206, no. 14; Le Roy, p. 236, no. 2; Dunand, no. 1621; Breccia, p. 23, no. 20; Pridik, p. 4, nos. 54—55; Šelov 1975, nos. 20—21; Gramatopol-Poenaru Bordea, Tomis, p. 56, no. 40; Lazarov 1977, p. 23, no. 16; Porro, p. 383, no. 27; Gentili, p. 45, no. 42; Brugnone, p. 71, no. 112.

18. Inv. no. 5/1981

Villa of Theseus, found in the baulk between sectors IV and V/81, above the level of the latitudinal wall

Dimensions: 4×0.4 cm

’Επὶ ’Αναξι-
βούλου
Καρνείου

Stamp of the eponym Anaxiboulos, month Karneios. See no. 17 above.

19. Inv. no. 17/1987

Late Hellenistic House, western part of sector 4/87, in the loose stone debris of a wall

Dimensions: 4.5×1.7 cm

Rectangular stamp with three lines of inscription:

’Επὶ ’Αρατο-
φάνευς
‘Υακινθίου

The same name is used by two Rhodian eponyms: Aratophanes I was active in period III as the finds from Pergamon prove[53], Aratophanes II is well placed by the finds of stamps with his name in Alba Fucens[54]. Our stamp should rather be connected with the first of the two. Grace believes him to have held his office sometime after 181 B.C.[55] Such producers as the Nysios mentioned above and Agoranax and Aristion[56], who cooperated with Aratophanes, appear to confirm her suggestion.

Stamps with the name of Aratophanes are a highly popular category in the archaeological record[57].

[53] Schuchhardt, pp. 444—445, nos. 867—873; see also Bleckmann 1912, p. 253, no. 43 — date 200—180 B.C.

[54] Mertens, p. 87, no. 9.

[55] Grace 1985, p. 8. See also Grace-Savvatianou, p. 297. The activity of Aratophanes falls in the period at the end of the 2nd cent. and beginning of 1st cent. B.C., see Grace-Savvatianou, p. 313, no. E 34, and p. 315, no. E 41.

[56] Bleckmann 1907, p. 32; Bleckmann 1912, p. 251; Badal’janc, p. 163; Benoit, p. 30, no. 3; Porro, p. 381, nos. 3—4; Porro 1916, p. 108

[57] Nilsson, no. 68; Grace 1934, no. 68; Grace 1953, p. 125; Grace 1956, nos. 102—103; Grace 1952, p. 528; Pridik, nos. 58—63; Šelov 1975, pp. 35—37, nos. 28—35; Levi 1964, nos. 49—51; Šelov 1956, p. 138, no. 62; Calvet 1978, p. 224, no. 8; Sztetyłło 1976, p. 37, nos. 51—52; Sztetyłło 1975, no. 228; Crowfoot, p. 380; Breccia, p. 25, no. 68; Gramatopol-Poenaru Bordea, Dacia XIII, no. 705.

20. Inv. no. 27/1988
Late Hellenistic House, in stone debris fill about 1 m down from the surface
Dimensions: 2.5 × 1.5 cm
'Επὶ 'Αρατο-
φάνευς
Πα[νάμου]

Stamp of eponym Aratophanes I, month Panamos. See no. 19 above.

21. Inv. no. 29/1978
Villa of Theseus, northern wing, upper layer
Diam: 3 cm
['Επὶ 'Αρατοφάνευς]? rose

The stamp is tentatively connected with the name of the eponym Aratophanes on the basis of a small subsidiary stamp with the letter "T". On the basis of three such preserved objects, Šelov associated this secondary stamp with the activity of the eponyms Aratophanes, Aristratos and Leontidas[58].

22. Inv. no. 2/1987
Late Hellenistic House, sector 1/87 just south of room R.48 of the Villa of Theseus, upper layer
Dimensions: 4.5 × 2 cm
Rectangular stamp with a three-line inscription:
'Επὶ 'Αριστα-
νάκτος
Καρνείου

The name of Aristanax is not often encountered on stamps of Rhodian origin and it has not been recorded in well dated archaeological assemblages. Grace places his activity in period V, mainly on the grounds of the characteristics of this stamp which are similar to those of this chronological group[59].

Finds come from Lindos, Delos and Egypt among others[60].

[58] See Šelov 1956, p. 138, no. 14.
[59] Grace 1952, p. 528.
[60] Loc. cit. and Nilsson, no. 78; Breccia, p. 25; Crowfoot, p. 381; Breccia, *BSAA* 9, 1907, p. 76, no. 60.

23. Inv. no. 11/1987
Villa of Theseus, western wing, west of room 16, in the northeastern part of sector 9/87, upper layer (ca. 1.25—1.50 m down from the surface)
Dimensions: 4.5×2 cm
Rectangular stamp with a three-line inscription:
Ἐπὶ Ἀριστο-
δάμου
Δαλίου

According to Grace there were two Rhodian eponyms of this name. Aristodamos I was active in the 3rd cent. B.C., while Aristodamos II in the second decade of the 2nd cent B.C.[61]. Our stamp belongs to Aristodamos II who filled his duties between 182 and 176 B.C. Such Rhodian producers as Hippokrates, Iason, Philainios and perhaps Nanis are to be connected with this eponym[62]. Amphorae stamped with the name of Aristodamos II have a characteristic subsidiary stamp, while the eponym used both rectangular and circular stamps[63].

Finds of stamps of Aristodamos have been recorded in many regions, i.e. in Pergamon, Delos, Rhodes, Tarsus, the Black Sea coast and areas of the ancient Near East to name some[64].

24. Inv. no. 3/1987
Late Hellenistic House, trench 1/87 located south of room 48 of the Villa of Theseus, in a layer above the preserved top of the latitudinal wall
Dimensions: 4×1.5 cm
Rectangular stamp with a three-line inscription:
Ἐπὶ Ἀριστομ-
βροτίδα
Ἀρταμιτίου

The activity of the eponym Aristombrotidas falls in period V[65]. This dating is confirmed, in V. Grace's opinion, by the concurrence of stamps of the producer Philostephanos who appears toge-

[61] Grace 1985, p. 8; Grace-Savvatianou, p. 291.
[62] Bleckmann 1907, pp. 31—32; Grace 1985, pp. 45—46 note 3. The author cites an amphora from Cyprus, stamped with the name of the potter Hippokrates and the eponym Theaidetos (contemporary to Aristodamos) and a small subsidiary stamp. The combination: Aristodamos — Philainios is mentioned by Nicolaou-Empereur, p. 518, no. 4. For the combination: Aristodamos — Nanis, see Grace-Savvatianou, p. 304, no. E 11.
[63] Reisner, p. 315, no. 7.
[64] Schuchhardt, pp. 447—449, nos. 895—914; Grace 1952, p. 528; Grace 1950, p. 141, no. 28; Šelov 1975, nos. 52—55; Sztetyłło 1983, no. 30; Pridik, nos. 76—81; Gramatopol-Poenaru Bordea, Dacia XIII, no. 710; Canarache, no. 672; Sztetyłło 1990, no. 17; Breccia, p. 26; Crowfoot, p. 381.
[65] Grace 1952, p. 528.

ther with other eponyms of period V, such as Chrysaon, Agoranax, Aischinas and Aristopolis[66]. Another Rhodian producer of period V whose stamps occur together with the stamps of Aristombrotidas and of Aischinas, and perhaps also with those of Aristopolis, Archibios and Archinos, was the producer Menestratos[67].

Stamps with the name of Aristombrotidas are not frequent in the archaeological record[68].

25. Inv. no. 4/1989
Villa of Theseus, sector 4/89, in secondary fill in place of robbed blocks
Dimensions: 3.7 × 1.5 cm
'Επὶ 'Αριστομ-
βροτίδα
Δαλίου

Stamp of the eponym Aristombrotidas, month Dalios. See no. 24 above.

26. Inv. no. 2/1982
Villa of Theseus, northern wing, upper layer of sector 2/82
Dimensions: 4.5 × 1.8 cm
Rectangular stamp with a three-line inscription:
'Επὶ 'Αρισ-
τονόμου
Πα [νάμου]

There is a lack of more certain data on the activity period of the eponym Aristonomos for his stamps have not been found in well-dated assemblages. Grace is of the opinion that he belongs to period V, maybe even to period IV, that is the middle of the 2nd cent B.C.[69].

Stamps of Aristonomos are known from only a few sites[70].

[66] Grace-Savvatianou, p. 312, no. E 33.
[67] Grace-Savvatianou, p. 296 and note 2. Grace mentions an amphora from Samaria, presently in the Museum in Jerusalem, with the stamps of the eponym Aristombrotidas and the producer Menestratos.
[68] See above and Nilsson, no. 106; Grace 1952, p. 528; Šelov 1975, nos. 57—59; Sztetyłło 1976, p. 61, no 175; Breccia, pp. 26—27; Crowfoot, p. 381.
[69] Grace 1954, p. 528; Grace-Savvatianou, p. 312, no. E 33 (chronological period V or VI).
[70] As above and Nilsson, no. 109; Breccia, p. 27.

27. Inv. no. 5/1978
Villa of Theseus, southern wing, near the mosaic of Achilles, upper layer
Dimensions: 4 × 1.7 cm
'Επὶ 'Αριστοπόλ-
ιος
Δα[λίου]

Eponym Aristopolis, month Dalios. Grace places the activity of this eponym in period V, that is the second half of the 2nd cent B.C.[71]. His stamps are fairly widespread, being found on Rhodes, Delos, Cyprus, the Black Sea coast and in Alexandria[72].

28. Inv. no. 20/1986
House of Aion, room 3, layer IV (ca 1.20—1.95 m down from the surface)
Dimensions: 4 × 1.7 cm
Rectangular stamp with a three-line inscription, using a lunate *sigma*.
'Επὶ 'Αρισ-
τράτου
Πεταγε(ιτνίου)

The rare stamps with the name of the eponym Aristratos are dated by V. Grace to the period before 150 B.C.[73] D.B. Šelov suggests the second half of the 2nd cent B.C. in view of the concurrence of small subsidiary stamps and the use of cursive on some of this eponym's stamps, both features especially common in the second half of the 2nd cent B.C.[74]. His activity is tentatively connected with that of the producer Hippokrates, working in the end of period III and at the beginning of period IV; another known combination is with the eponym Aristratos and the producer Rhodon II[75].

As mentioned above, stamps of this eponym are not very numerous[76].

[71] Grace-Savvatianou, p. 296 and 312, no. E 33.
[72] Nilsson, no. 11; Paris 1914, pp. 304—305, XVIII; Grace 1952, p. 528; Grace 1953, p. 122, no. 50; Sztetyłło 1976, nos. 176—180; Sztetyłło 1984, no. 13; Šelov 1975, nos. 60—61; Breccia, p. 27; Sztetyłło 1975, nos. 119—120; Empereur 1977, no 19; Sztetyłło 1983, no. 85; Crowfoot, p. 381.
[73] Grace 1952, p. 528; Grace 1953, p. 122; Grace-Savvatianou, no. E 45.
[74] Šelov 1975, nos. 63—65; Šelov 1956, p. 144.
[75] Badal'janc, p. 164. For the activity of Hippokrates see cat. no. 61. For the combination: Aristratos — producer Rhodon II, see Nicolaou-Empereur, pp. 523—524, no. 8.
[76] As above and Nilsson, p. 190, no. 113; I. Nicolaou, *RDAC* 1970, p. 159, no. 20; Pridik, p. 6, no. 91; Šelov 1975, nos. 63—65; Šelov 1956, p. 144; Lazarov 1977, p. 25, no. 31; Breccia, p. 27; Crowfoot, p. 381.

29. Inv. no. Ip/1981
Villa of Theseus, surface find
Dimensions: 4 × 1.4 cm
'Επὶ 'Αρχε[μβρ]ότου
'Αρταμιτίου

Of the two eponyms of this name, Archembrotos I was active in period V and Archembrotos II in period IV[77]. Brugnone quotes the view of some researchers who considered the two Archembrotoi to have been the father and son of a priestess named Hageso known from a dedicatory inscription from Ialysssos from 68 B.C.[78] Our stamp seems to be that of Archembrotos II who worked together with producers Menandros and Stephanos[79].

Stamps of both eponyms are common[80].

30. Inv. no. IP/1981
Surface find from the vicinity of the Villa of Theseus
Dimensions: 4 × 1.7 cm
['Επὶ 'Αρ]χιβίου
'Υ[ακιν]θίου

Stamp of the eponym Archibios, month Hyakinthios.

Archibios' activity is placed by Grace in period V, that is at the end of the 2nd cent. B.C.[81], mainly on the grounds of finds from Alba Fucens[82] and Rhodes[83]. He cooperated with the producer Menestratos just as two other eponyms of the period, Aristopolis and Archinos[84], did.

Stamps of Archibios are not frequent[85].

[77] Grace 1952, p. 529; Grace 1965, p. 15; Grace-Savvatianou, p. 315, E 40.
[78] Brugnone, p. 30, no. 11, notes 76—77.
[79] Grace 1953, p. 119 and no. 7; Grace 1965, p. 14, fig. 3a, p. 115, D-E; Grace-Savvatianou, p. 315, E 40, and Grace 1962, p. 117, no. 11.
[80] Nilsson, no. 131; Grace 1952, p. 529; Grace-Savvatianou, p. 315, E 40; Sztetyłło 1976, no. 221; Pridik, no. 101; Sztetyłło 1983, nos. 89—90; Macalister, p. 354; Reisner, p. 313; Crowfoot, p. 381; Sztetyłło 1975, nos. 160—162; Sztetyłło 1978, no. 49; Sztetyłło 1990, nos. 92—93; Brugnone, no. 11; Le Roy, no. 5; Breccia, p. 28.
[81] Grace-Savvatianou, p. 296 and no. E 33.
[82] Mertens, no. 18.
[83] Paris 1914, pp. 300—326.
[84] Grace-Savvatianou, p. 296.
[85] Mertens, no. 18; Paris 1914, pp. 306—307, XI; Grace 1952, p. 529f.; Šelov 1975, nos. 73—76; Sztetyłło 1975, no. 122; Sztetyłło 1990, no. 94; Crowfoot, p. 381; Le Roy, no. 6.

31. Inv. no. IP/1981

Surface find from the vicinity of the Villa of Theseus

Dimensions: 4 × 1.7 cm

'Επὶ 'Αρχιδά-
μου
Δαλίου

A three-line stamp of the eponym Archidamos, month Dalios.

Archidamos is dated to ca 192 B.C.[86] One producer he cooperated with was Sokrates[87] who also worked with the eponyms Sostratos[88] and Symmachos[89]. At first Grace dated his activity to period III in general[90], but later she corrected this to ca 192 B.C.[91] on the basis of the finds from Pergamon. One find is of special importance in this case. It is the presence of a small subsidiary stamp on an amphora of Symmachos; the stamp, in the form of a blooming rose, reflects a habit started around 188 B.C. by the producer Damokrates. This dates Symmachos' activity to the second decade of the 2nd cent. B.C.[92] Therefore, Archidamos should be placed in the period ca 190—180 B.C.

Stamps of this eponym are not frequently encountered[93].

32a

32. Inv. no. 19/1986

House of Aion, room 3, layer 5 (ca 1.5 m down from the surface)

Diam.: 3 cm

Circular stamp with a representation of a rose in the centre and an inscription running around it. A small subsidiary stamp "IC", impressed on the underside of the handle.

'Επὶ 'Αρχιλαίδα [rose

[86] Grace 1974, p. 199.
[87] Grace, Kyme 1, p. 95, no. A 4.
[88] Grace-Savvatianou, no. E 3 and E 5, pl. 53.
[89] Grace, Kyme 1, p. 96, no. A 4.
[90] Grace-Savvatianou, p. 371, no. 4.
[91] Loc. cit.
[92] Grace 1974, p. 199.
[93] Grace 1985, pp. 8—9 and 45, 1; Schuchhardt, no. 944; Nilsson, no. 134 (4 examples); Grace 1952, p. 529f.; Levi 1964, nos. 62—66; Sztetyłło 1976, no. 68; Calvet 1978, nos. 11—12; Calvet 1982, no. 36; Breccia, p. 29; Sztetyłło 1990, nos. 19—20; Levi, Iasos, p. 549, no. 10.

32b

Assuming the stamp was read correctly, it should be considered as a stamp of the eponym Archilaidas. This name is known from the Pergamon assemblage[94]. A concurrence with the stamps of the producer Aristokles, one of the most active Rhodian producers[95], permits a closer dating of this eponym. According to Grace, Archilaidas held his office in the period 182—176 B.C.[96]

Very frequent, stamps of the eponym Archilaidas are met with in many regions[97].

33. Inv. no. 1/1985
Villa of Theseus, western wing, western end of room 17, upper layer
Dimensions: 2.8 × 1.7 cm
Rectangular stamp with a double-line legend. Neat lettering.
'Επὶ 'Αρχοκ-
ράτ [ευς]   head of Helios

The eponym Archokrates was recorded in the Pergamon assemblage[98]. Another well-dated group in which his stamps were noted was the material from Villanova[99] where they concurred with stamps of the producer Aristos. Nachtergael draws attention to the great variety of this eponym's stamps[100] and he does not exclude the possibility of there having been another eponym of this name[101], active in period IV. The Archokrates known from Rhodian stamps is tentatively identified by Blinkenberg with one Archokrates Archipolios who came from a Rhodian family of priests and who was priest in Lindos in the last quarter of the 3rd cent. B.C.[102] Preserved Rhodian amphora bear examples of the concurrence of the stamps of Archokrates with stamps of such Rhodian produ-

[94] Schuchhardt, nos. 960—966.
[95] See Nilsson, no. 135; Nicolaou-Empereur, p. 519, no. 5 (with a small subsidiary stamp B). For the combination Archilaidas — Aristokles, see Pridik, p. 26, no. 107; Šelov 1975, p. 88, no. 288 and p. 45, no. 77; Grace 1949, p. 187, pls. 19.5 and 20.4—5; Grace-Savvatianou, p. 279 note 2 and p. 291 note 3; Grace 1985, pp. 11, 17, and 23, no. 61; Badal'janc, p. 164. For the activity of the potter Aristokles see our cat. no. 93.
[96] Grace 1985, pp. 8—11.
[97] See notes 54—56 above and Nilsson, no. 135; Grace 1934, no. 59; Grace 1952, p. 528; Šelov 1975, nos. 77—78; Levi 1964, nos. 67—74; Sztetyłło 1976, nos. 146—148; Breccia, p. 29; Sztetyłło 1975, no. 58; Empereur 1977, no. 23; Sztetyłło 1990, no. 20; Crowfoot, p. 381.
[98] Schuchhardt, nos. 967—977.
[99] Maiuri, p. 258, XXVII—XXVIII. Stamps of Aristos were also found in Pergamon, see Schuchhardt, no. 960 and 967—977. See also Gaertringen, Rhodos, 837, no. 97. Grace places Archokrates in period III, see Grace 1952, p. 528 and Grace-Savvatianou, p. 294; Grace 1953, p. 122, no. 61.
[100] Nachtergael, p. 39, no. 13.
[101] Nachtergael, p. 40, note 6.
[102] Blinkenberg II, 1, 23, 35, 115, 379, and Blinkenberg, "Lindiaka VI", *Archeologisk Kunsthistoriske Meddelser* II, 2, København 1937, pp. 21, 11, 101—102, and p. 27, no. 32 and p. 28.

cers as Dokimos, Marsyas and Philainios, all belonging to period III[103].

Stamps of Archokrates are frequently recorded among the finds from various archaeological sites[104].

34. Inv. no. 31/1987
Late Hellenistic House, sector 13/87, upper layer
Diam.: 3 cm
Circular stamp with a rose representation and an inscription around it:

'Επὶ 'Αρχοκράτευς 'Υακινθίου rose

Stamp of the eponym Archokrates. See no. 33 above.

35. Inv. no. 6/1989
Late Hellenistic House, above the level of the cistern in the upper layer
Dimensions: 6×2.2 cm

['Επὶ] Αὐτοκρά-
τευς
'Ερμαίου

Eponym Autokrates, producer Hermaios. An analogous stamp with the names of both the eponym Autokrates and the producer Hermaios is given by Nilsson[105]. Autokrates cooperated also with other producers of period IV: Imas known from many stamps[106], the equally popular Bromios[107] and quite probably Drakontidas[108]. Grace places his activity in the years 175—146 B.C.[109] The producer Hermaios was considered a producer of period VI, but the name is known from earlier times, including the period after 188 B.C.[110] The combination of eponym Archembrotos — with — Hermaios quoted by Nilsson makes it possible to date at least one producer of this name to period IV, in which we have the eponym Archembrotos II, or to period V in which there was Archembrotos I[111]. Our stamp may be dated

[103] Grace 1934, p. 219; Pridik 1926, pp. 311, 320, 323; Gentili, p. 28; Badal'janc, p. 164.
[104] See above and Nilsson, no. 137; Porro 1916, p. 113, no. 51; Paris 1914, p. 158, XXIX; Grace 1952, p. 529; Grace 1953, no. 31; Calvet 1972, no. 35; I. Nicolaou, *RDAC* 1967, p. 84, no. 8f; Sztetyłło 1976, p. 40, no. 69; Pridik, p. 7, nos. 110—112; Levi 1964, p. 264, no. 75; Lazarov 1977, p. 26, no. 37; Sztetyłło 1983, pp. 80—81, nos. 37—41; Nachtergael, no. 13; Empereur 1977, p. 209, no. 24; Sztetyłło 1975, p. 177, nos. 59—60; Sztetyłło 1978, p. 273, no. 22; Reisner, p. 314; Macalister, p. 355; Crowfoot, p. 381; Börker, p. 36, no. 8; Brugnone, pp. 13—14, nos. 12—14; Le Roy, BIFAO 84, p. 309, no. 4.
[105] Nilsson, p. 404, no. 142, 2.
[106] Badal'janc, p. 165; Grace, Amphoras, fig. 31; Grace-Savvatianou, p. 304.
[107] Börker, no. 85.
[108] Gentili, no. 19. See also Nachtergael, p. 40.
[109] Grace 1952, p. 529.
[110] Grace-Savvatianou, no. E 20 and E 21.
[111] Nilsson, p. 420, no. 196, 4.

after 188 B.C., quite possibly right down to the beginning of period V (a long period of activity by Imas?), not only on the basis of the concurrence of the name of Autokrates with that of producers of the period 175—146 B.C. who cooperated also with other eponyms known after the year 188 B.C., but also on the grounds of small secondary stamps used by Autokrates[112], stamps which were introduced by Damokrates around 188 B.C.

Autokrates' stamps do not occur very often in the material from excavations[113].

36a

36b

36. Inv. no. IP/1981
Villa of Theseus, near the western wing
Diam.: 3.2 cm
'Επὶ Γόργωνος 'Υακινθίου rose

Stamp of the eponym Gorgon with a small subsidiary stamp. Rarely found, stamps of this eponym have not been recorded in any of the well-dated assemblages, thus encumbering all attempts at dating him. Grace places him in period IV[114], but it is more probably the second half of the 2nd cent. B.C. that should be considered in view of the producers that appear together with him: Bromios[115] and Diokleias[116], whose activity continued into period V. Nilsson's attempt at assigning a fragmentarily preserved stamp with just the end of the name of the eponym and the name of the producer Antigonos to the eponym Gorgon does not appear sufficiently credible[117]. Further evidence in favour of dating Gorgon to the second half of the 2nd cent. B.C. constitute the small subsidiary stamps introduced about 188 B.C. and made especially common after 150 B.C.[118]

As said already, stamps of this eponym are not a frequent find[119].

[112] Šelov 1975, nos. 88—95.
[113] Nilsson, no. 142; Grace 1952, p. 529; Pridik, p. 7, no. 120; Gramatopol-Poenaru Bordea, Dacia XIII, no. 714; Šelov 1975, nos. 88—95; Sztetyłło 1990, p. 178, no. 38. See also R. Étienne, "La date du prêtre de Rhodes, Autocrates", *BCH* Suppl. XIII, 1986, pp. 45—47; Crowfoot, p. 381.
[114] Grace 1952, p. 529; Grace 1950, no. 42.
[115] L. Jalabert — R. Mouterde *Les inscriptions grecques et latins de la Syrie* V, Paris 1959, p. 103, no. 2188 b.
[116] Porro, p. 382, nos. 7—8.
[117] Nilsson, p. 104 note 2. See Nachtergael, p. 43 note 4.
[118] Šelov 1956, p. 138, no. 25.
[119] Nilsson, no. 151, Paris 1914, p. 307, XXVI; Grace 1950, no. 42; Grace 1952, p. 529; Šelov 1975, no. 95; Crowfoot, p. 381; Breccia, p. 30.

37. Inv. no. 18/1987
Late Hellenistic House, sector 4/87, upper layer
Dimensions: 4 × 1.5 cm
Rectangular stamp with a double-line inscription:
'Επὶ Δαμαινέτου
Δαλίου

Stamp of the eponym Damainetos, considered by Grace to be an eponym of period IV, that is of the first half of the 2nd cent. B.C.[120] The presence of these stamps in Carthage[121] and a total lack of them in Pergamon speak in favour of such a dating. According to Grace, Damainetos was contemporary to such eponyms as Pausanias III and Timourrodos from period IV[122]. The stamps of Damainetos are characterized by a great variety; he uses both kinds of stamps, rectangular and circular[123]. Small subsidiary stamps accompany sometimes the stamps with the name of Damainetos[124]. He cooperated with one of the most active producers of the time, Imas[125].

Finds of this eponym's stamps were recorded in the Mediterranean region, the ancient Near East and on the Black Sea coast[126].

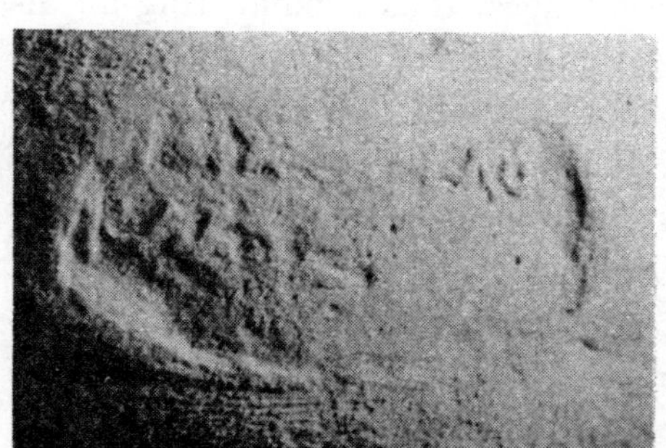

38. Inv. no. 5/1981
Villa of Theseus, pottery deposit in sector I/81
Dimensions: 4.1 × 1.6 cm
'Επὶ Δαμο-
κλεῦς

Eponym Damokles or Charmokles.

It seems that there were two eponyms of this name on Rhodes. Damokles I was probably active in the second half of the 3rd cent. B.C.[127] and Damokles II in period III as proven by stamps of his found in the Pergamon deposit and on the Agora[128]. Grace emphasizes the difficulties in dating both eponyms and the resulting differences in determinations of their periods of activity[129]. One of the producers appearing together with Damokles II (for it is to him that our stamp should be attributed) is Marsyas who is known from many

[120] Grace 1952, p. 529; Grace-Savvatianou, p. 304, no. E 7.
[121] Gaertringen, Rhodos, no. 107.
[122] Grace-Savvatianou, p. 304, no. E 7.
[123] Säfflund, no. 19 (circular); Šelov 1975, nos. 96—98 (rectangular).
[124] Reisner, p. 315, no. 8.
[125] Grace-Savvatianou, p. 304, no. E 7.
[126] As above and Nilsson, no. 159; Grace 1952, p. 529; Pridik, no. 136; Šelov 1975, nos. 96—98; Levi, Festos, no. 1; Sztetyłło 1975, no. 102; Sztetyłło 1990, no. 40; Säfflund, no. 19; Börker, no. 25; Crowfoot, p. 381; Empereur 1977, no. 23.
[127] Grace 1974, p. 197.
[128] Grace 1985, p. 44.
[129] Grace 1985, p. 12 note 23 and p. 44; Grace-Savvatianou, p. 290 note 5.

stamps assigned to the end of period III and the beginning of period IV[130]. Charmokles is placed in period II.

Stamps of Damokles are not frequent finds in the archaeological record[131].

39. Inv. no. IP/1981
Villa of Theseus, sector IV/81, upper layer
Dimensions: 4.1 × 1.3 cm
'Επὶ Δαμοκλεῦς
Βαδρομίου

Stamp of the eponym Damokles II, month Badromios. See no. 38 above.

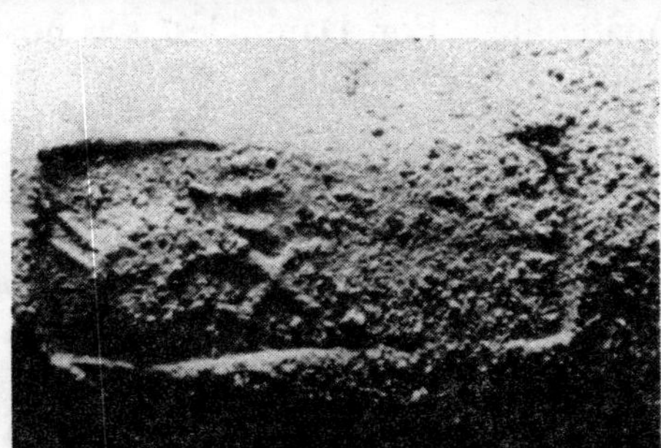

40. Inv. no. 35/1986
Villa of Theseus, southern wing, surface find
Dimensions: 3.5 × 1.5 cm
Rectangular stamp with two lines of inscription. On the left a representation of the head of Helios.
'Επὶ Δορ- head of Helios
χυλίδα

One example of a stamp of eponym Dorchylidas was found in Pergamon[132] and on these grounds he was placed in period III[133]. A more exact dating took into account the concurrence of Dorchylidas' name on amphorae stamped by Rhodian producers, primarily Aristion[134]. Aristion's name has been preserved in the Pergamon material[135] and his appearing together with other eponyms of this period has made it possible to narrow down his years to 210—175 B.C.[136]

Stamps of Dorchylidas were found in Rhodes, Delos, Cyprus, Egypt and on the coast of the Black Sea[137].

[130] Bleckmann 1907, p. 32; Bleckmann 1912, p. 251; Badal'janc, p. 165.

[131] Schuchhardt, nos. 980—996; Nilsson, no. 165; Grace 1952, p. 529; Grace 1934, no. 42; Grace 1953, no. 70; Sztetyłło 1976, nos. 75—76; Levi 1964, nos. 77—87; Breccia, p. 31; Empereur 1977, no. 28; Sztetyłło 1975, nos. 62—63. Charmokles, cf. Grace 1952, p. 530; Brugnone, no. 59.

[132] Schuchhardt, no. 1010.

[133] Grace 1985, p. 40. See also Grace 1952, p. 529; Grace 1953, p. 122, no. 74; Bleckmann 1912, p. 215, no. 106; Gaertringen, Rhodos, 837, no. 120.

[134] Paris, p. 325; Badal'janc, p. 164.

[135] Schuchhardt, nos. 891—892.

[136] The following eponyms belonged to them: Kleitomachos, Kleukrates and Aratophanes I. For the combination Aristion-Kleitomachos, see Benoit, p. 29, no. 1. For a concurrence of the names Aristion and the eponym Kleukrates, see Gentili, pp. 27, 34, no. 6. Stamps related to the names of Aristion and the eponym Aratophanes I, see Benoit, p. 30, no. 3. Brugnone, p. 18, no. 20 and p. 48, no. 68, mentions another combination: Aristion — the eponym Theudoros. The author quotes Grace who dates Theudoros to period II. The attempt to identify Theudoros with Theudoros Xenophantos of 248 B.C. or with Theudoros Onesandros of 220 B.C. would confirm Grace's suggestion concerning the activity of Dorchylidas, a contemporary of Aristion; she would see it at the beginning of period III, possibly at the end of period II.

[137] Nillsson, no. 183; Paris, p. 160, XXXVII; Paris 1914, p. 324; Grace 1952, p. 529; Calvet 1978, no. 19; Calvet 1982, p. 23, no. 44; Sztetyłło 1976, p. 43, nos. 87—88; Empereur 1977, nos. 38—40; Sztetyłło 1975, no. 68; Šelov 1975, nos. 100—101: Sztetyłło 1990, no. 23; Crowfoot, p. 381. See also notes 72—74 above.

41. Inv. no. 11/1978
Villa of Theseus, layer 2 inside well SW 80/1978
Dimensions: 3 × 1.5 cm
['Επὶ Εὐκ-]
λεῦς
Θεσμοφορίου

Eukles or Damokles.

The stamp has been tentatively reconstructed on the basis of the fragmentarily preserved inscription and the characteristic features of the handle. Grace considers the eponym Eukles one of a group of early eponyms from the period 240—225 B.C., in which the names of the eponyms are accompanied by the names of months[138]. The stamps of Eukles as well as the stamps of other eponyms of this period, sometimes lacking the official titles, are not often encountered in the material[139]. For Damokles, see nos 38—39 above.

42. Inv. no. IP/1979
From the neighbourhood of the Villa of Theseus
Dimensions: 4.3 × 2 cm
'Επὶ [Ε]ὐάνορος
Θευδαισίου

Surface of the stamp partly destroyed. Stamp with name of the eponym Euanor, month Theudaisios. The eponym Euanor is attributed to period V[140]. His stamps were found in Rhodes[141], Tarsus[142], the Black Sea coast[143], Egypt and Cyprus[144].

43. Inv. no. 39/1977
Villa of Theseus, western part, upper layer of sector W. 80 (area of the so-called "octagonal" tower)
Dimensions: 3.7 × 1.2 cm
['Επὶ 'Ηραγ-]
όρα
Δαλίου

The eponym Heragoras is attributed to period IV[145], although there are some difficulties in pinpointing him exactly. There are no stamps of this eponym in the Pergamon group; there are, how-

[138] Group II A, Grace-Savvatianou, p. 301; See also Grace 1963, p. 324 note 12, and p. 326 note 16. Also Grace 1974, p. 197 and 200. Also Nicolaou-Empereur, p. 516, no. 1; Brugnone, p. 86 note 508.
[139] Nilsson, no. 205; Grace 1952, pp. 523, 529, 537, nos. 14—15, pl. XXI; Grace 1956, no. 76; Pridik, no. 162; Šelov 1975, no. 111.
[140] Grace 1952, p. 529; Grace 1953, no. 78.
[141] Nilsson, no. 200; Paris 1914, p. 309.
[142] Grace 1950, no. 43.
[143] Šelov 1975, nos. 106—109.
[144] Empereur 1977, no. 44; Calvet 1978, no. 23.
[145] Grace 1952, p. 529.

ever, stamps of the producer Marsyas[146] with whom Heragoras cooperated[147] and whose activity started most probably at the beginning of the 2nd cent. B.C.[148] Grace notes that in the Benachi collection in Alexandria there is a stamp of Heragoras made with a die remodelled from a die of the eponym Aristomachos[149], who however is also uncertainly dated[150]. Some of the stamps of Heragoras are accompanied by small subsidiary stamps[151] introduced around 188 B.C., but made common only in the second half of the 2nd cent. B.C. Thus, it would seem that Heragoras became active, similarly to Marsyas, at the end of period III, that is at the start of the 2nd cent. B.C. and continued being active slightly into the second half of the century, that is already in period IV (ca. 175—146 B.C.)[152].

Stamps of Heragoras have been recorded in Rhodes, Delos, Cyprus, the Black Sea coast and Egypt[153].

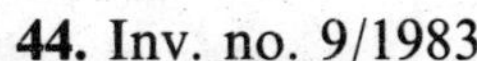

44. Inv. no. 9/1983
Villa of Theseus, northern wing, sector 10/82/83
Diam.: 3 cm
Circular stamp with a representation of a rose in the centre and legend:
'Επὶ Θέστορος 'Αγριανίου

Stamps with the name of the eponym Thestor were found in well-dated complexes such as Pergamon and Carthage[154]. This enabled Grace to date him to the end of the 3rd cent.B.C.[155] His stamps are accompanied by the stamps of the following producers of the period: Aristeidas[156], Aristokrates[157] and Dios[158].

Stamps of Thestor are encountered on many archaeological sites[159].

[146] Schuchhardt, nos. 1127—1134.
[147] Sztetyłło 1976, no. 92 and 109.
[148] Nicolaou-Empereur, p. 516, no. 2 and p. 533.
[149] Grace-Savvatianou, p. 314, no. E 37.
[150] Above and also Šelov 1975, no. 56.
[151] Šelov 1956, no. 21; Šelov 1975, no. 114.
[152] Brugnone, no. 96 — stamps of Marsyas and eponyms cooperating with him.
[153] Nilsson, no. 223; Grace 1952, p. 529; Sztetyłło 1976, nos. 92—93; Šelov 1975, nos. 114—116; Mirčev, no. 92; Breccia, no. 34; Sztetyłło 1975, no. 103; Sztetyłło 1990, no. 48; Börker, no. 16. See also Gaertringen, Rhodos, no. 145, and Bleckmann 1912, no. 128.
[154] Schuchhardt, nos. 1032—1035. See also Grace 1952, p. 529; Grace-Savvatianou, p. 294.
[155] Grace-Savvatianou, p. 294; Grace 1963, p. 325.
[156] Badal'janc, p. 164; Paris, p. 172.
[157] Brugnone, p. 18 note 123. See Paris, p. 172; Badal'janc, p. 164; Börker, p. 35, no. 6; Pridik, nos. 511—515.
[158] Grace 1963, p. 334, nos. 9; Grace, Amphoras, fig. 62; Grace-Savvatianou, p. 294; Badal'janc, p. 164. See also Šelov 1975, p. 96 note 505.
[159] Nilsson, no. 236; Paris 1914, p. 310, XLVII; Grace 1952, p. 529; Levi, Iasos, p. 551, no. 15; Levi-Pugliese Caratelli, p. 612, no. 26; Grace 1934, p. 229, no. 53; Grace 1963, p. 334, no. 9; Sztetyłło 1976, no. 98; Pridik, p. 10, nos. 181—188 and p. 133, nos. 34—34; Šelov 1975, no. 119; Mirčev, no. 94; Lazarov 1977, p. 28, no. 59; Lazarov 1974, p. 48, no. 52; Macalister, p. 358; Reisner, p. 313; Crowfoot, p. 381; Brugnone, pp. 17—18, no. 19; Gentili, p. 64, no. 109; Pellegrini, p. 231, nos. 269—270.

45. Inv. no. 30/1980

Villa of Theseus, northeastern part of the building, surface find

Dimensions: 4×1.3 cm

Legend: [᾿Επὶ ῾Ιέ]ρωνος solar disc

Of the two Rhodian eponyms of this name, Hieron I was active in period III (ca 210—175 B.C.)[160] and Hieron II in period V (148—108 B.C.) and period VI (108—80 B.C.)[161], to put it more exactly, at the end of period V and beginning of period VI, at which time he stamped concurrently with Agathoboulos. The shape of the handle and the type of emblem suggests the stamp to be one of Hieron I, although the form of the stamps and the one-line inscription are close to the rarely encountered stamps of Hieron II[162].

Stamps of Hieron I were found in the Pergamon assemblage[163], but his activity seems to fall in the very end of the "Pergamene" period, that is in the beginning of the 2nd cent. B.C. In favour of such a dating are the stamps of Hieron and Diskos found in Villanova[164], the context of the finds from Tarsus[165] and the use of a small subsidiary stamp[166]. Apart from his cooperation with Diskos II, Hieron I accompanied with his stamp those of such producers as Antigonos[167], Antimachos[168], Aristokrates[169], Damophilos[170] and Sokrates[172].

Contrary to the rare stamps of Hieron II, the stamps of Hieron I appear to be one of the more frequent stamps found on various archaeological sites[173].

[160] Grace 1952, p. 529; See also Nachtergael, p. 43, no. 16, and Grace-Savvatianou, p. 294; Grace 1985, p. 23 note 60=198.

[161] As above and also Grace-Savvatianou, p. 305, no. E 15.

[162] Grace-Savvatianou, loc. cit.; see also Gramatopol-Poenaru Bordea, Dacia XIII, no. 721.

[163] Schuchhardt, nos. 1040—1049.

[164] Maiuri, pp. 253—254, Ib—VIII and p. 263.

[165] Grace 1950, p. 136 and 144 and no. 71.

[166] Šelov 1956, no. 1 and Šelov 1975, p. 56.

[167] Badal'janc, p. 163; Schuchhardt, no. 1042; Bleckmann 1907, p. 33; Nilsson, p. 105 note 2, no. 253, 2; Crowfoot, p. 387.

[168] Gentili, no. 120, 13.

[169] Gentili, no. 3.

[170] Badal'janc, p. 164.

[171] As above.

[172] Schuchhardt, p. 426; Bleckmann 1907, p. 22 and 31; Badal'janc, p. 165.

[173] Schuchhardt, nos. 1040—1049; Nilsson, no. 253; Paris, p. 310, L; Grace 1952, p. 529; Grace 1950, no. 71; Pridik, nos. 200—207; Šelov 1975, nos. 122—125; Levi 1964, no. 107; Gramatopol-Poenaru Bordea, Dacia XIII, no. 721; Sztetyłło 1983, no. 63; Breccia, p. 37; Empereur 1977, nos. 61—62; Sztetyłło 1975, no. 99; Crowfoot, p. 381; Macalister, p. 358; Reisner, p. 313. For finds from Italy and Italian collections see Brugnone, nos. 27—32.

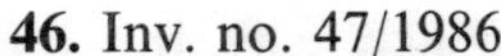

46. Inv. no. 47/1986
Villa of Theseus, southern wing, sector 1/P/86, below the level of the wall with preserved painted decoration
Dimensions: 4.5 × 1.5 cm
Rectangular stamp with three lines of inscription:
'Επὶ 'Ιέρω-
νος
Πανάμου

Stamp of eponym Hieron I(?), month Panamos. See no. 45 above.

47. Inv. no. 31/1982
Villa of Theseus, northern wing, together with Inv. no. 29/1982 and 30/1982, sector 15/82, upper layer
Dimensions: 3.5 × 1.7 cm
Rectangular stamps with two lines of inscription and a representation of the head of Helios to the left of the legend.
'Επὶ 'Ιασι-
κράτευς   head of Helios

The basically very variform stamps of the eponym Iasikrates were found in Pergamon and Villanova[147], dating this eponym generally to the end of the 3rd cent. B.C., furthermore confirmed by the concurrence of Iasikrates and the producer Agesilas among the finds from the Athenian Agora, recorded there in a context from the end of the 3rd cent. B.C.[175]

Stamps of Iasikrates are quite common in the archaeological record from various sites[176].

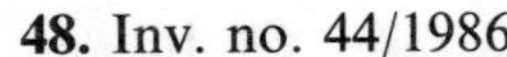

48. Inv. no. 44/1986
Villa of Theseus, southern wing, sector 3/86, upper layer
Dimensions: 2.5 × 1.5 cm
Rectangular stamp with a partially obliterated surface, two lines of inscription:
'Επὶ 'Ιάσονος
Σμινθίου

Stamps of the eponym Iason are not frequently encountered. Grace mentions one eponym of this name in period VI[177].

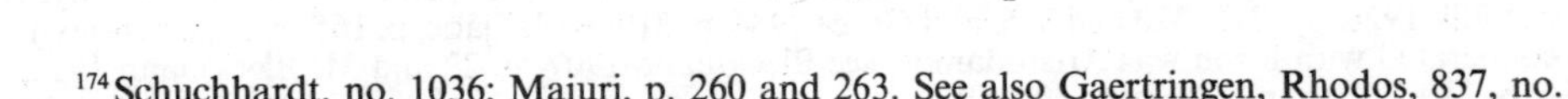

[174] Schuchhardt, no. 1036; Maiuri, p. 260 and 263. See also Gaertringen, Rhodos, 837, no. 172; Grace 1953, p. 129, no. 93.

[175] Badal'janc, p. 163. For a proposed combination Iasikrates — Agesilas, see Brugnone, no. 22 and no. 63. For a dating of Iasikrates and Agesilas, see Grace-Savvaniatou, p. 303, no. E 4 and E 5. For the archaeological context of the Komos cistern on the Athenian Agora, see Thompson, *Hesperia* 32, 1963, p. 276.

[176] Nilsson, no. 264; Paris 1914, p. 310, XLIX; Porro 1916, p. 116, no. 106; Grace 1952, p. 529; Calvet 1978, p. 225, no. 25; Calvet 1982, p. 25, nos. 55—56; I. Nicolaou, *RDAC* 1965, p. 116, 4 c; Pridik, p. 10, nos. 197—199 and p. 133, no. 38; Šelov 1975, no. 121; Lazarov 1977, p. 28; no. 63; Sztetyłło 1978, p. 269, no. 12; Empereur 1977, p. 219, no. 58; Macalister, p. 358; Crowfoot, p. 381; Gentili, p. 65, no. 115; Pellegrini, p. 246, no. 380.

[177] Grace-Savvatianou, pp. 315—316, no. E 42. One Iason, a producer, is known from three stamps in the

49. Inv. no. IP/1981
Villa of Theseus, sector V/81, on the level of the latitudinal wall
Dimensions: 3.6 × 1.5 cm
['Επὶ Καλ]λικρά-
τευς
[ ]ου

The reconstruction of the legend is tentative owing to the obliterated surface. It would appear that the eponym's name was Kallikrates and that the third line contained the name of the month. According to Grace there were three eponyms of this name active on Rhodes: Kallikrates I in period I, Kallikrates II in the so-called "Pergamene" period and Kallikrates III in period IV[178]. Our object seems to belong to the second of these, an eponym confirmed by stamps found at Pergamon[179]. Šelov believes that this eponym should be placed at the beginning of the 2nd cent. B.C., his cooperation with the producer Dios of this period being evidence for this[180]. Other producers whose stamps coincide with the stamps of this eponym include Damokrates[181] and possibly Soteridas[182].

Stamps of Kallikrates II are often found in the material[183].

50. Inv. no. 17/1978
Surface find from the Villa of Theseus
Diam.: 3 cm
['Επὶ Κ] αλλικράτευς [Δα]λίου head of Helios

Stamp of Kallikrates II. See no. 49 above.

Pergamon deposit, see Schuchhardt, nos. 1037—1039. The producer Iason cooperated with the eponym Kallikratidas II, see Pridik 1926, pp. 315, 320 and 325, and Grace 1934, p. 219; Badal'janc, p. 165. Another eponym of period III who cooperated with Iason was Aristodamos, see Bleckmann 1907, p. 22 and 31; Bleckmann 1912, p. 251; Grace 1934, p. 219; Porro, p. 386, nos. 49—50.

[178] Grace 1952, p. 525 and 529; Grace 1953, p. 118 note 5; Grace 1963, p. 324 note 12; Nachtergael, p. 52.

[179] Schuchhardt, nos. 1053—1062.

[180] Šelov 1975, p. 56, no. 124; Levi 1964, nos. 334—335, no. XXII.

[181] Gentili, no. 5.

[182] Pridik, no. 210; Pridik 1926, p. 314ff and 330; Badal'janc, p. 165.

[183] Nilsson, no. 263 (27 examples); Paris 1914, p. 310, LII; Grace 1952, p. 525 and 529; Grace 1934, no. 29; Grace 1950, nos. 74—75; Sztetyłło 1976, nos. 99—100; Sztetyłło 1984, no. 6; Šelov 1975, nos. 124—127; Mirčev, no. 99; Levi 1964, nos. 108—115; Breccia, p. 37; Nachtergael, no. 21; Sztetyłło 1975, nos. 83—85; Brugnone, no. 115(?); Säflund, no. 6; Crowfoot, p. 381.

51. Inv. no. 18/1986
House of Aion, room 3, layer 4 (ca 1.20—1.95 m down from the surface)
Diam.: 3 cm
Circular stamp with a representation of a rose and an inscription around it. Small, very fine lettering.
Ἐπὶ Καλλικρατίδα rose

Stamps with the name of Kallikratidas are connected with two eponyms. Kallikratidas I, who has less stamps in general, was active in the earliest period of the stamping of amphorae on Rhodes (period I)[184]. Kallikratidas II, whose stamps are of the more commonly encountered variety and were found in Pergamon as well, is to be placed in period III[185]. An analysis of the finds from the Athenian Agora has narrowed this down to 188—186 B.C.[186] The Paphos stamp belongs to this second eponym. His stamps appear together with the stamps of many producers of period III, including Damokrates, the person who according to Grace introduced the small subsidiary stamps around 188 B.C.[187]

As mentioned earlier, the stamps of Kallikratidas II are among the more common ones[188].

52. Inv. no. 17/1985
Villa of Theseus, western wing, upper layer of the baulk between sectors 2/85 and 3/85
Diam.: 3.2 cm
Circular stamp with a representation of a rose and an encircling legend:
Ἐπὶ Καλλικρατίδα rose

Stamp of the eponym Kallikratidas II. See no. 51 above.

[184] Grace 1952, p. 529.
[185] As above and Schuchhardt, nos. 1063—1081.
[186] Grace-Savvatianou, p. 291 and 295 note 1.
[187] Badal'janc, p. 164; Grace 1985, pp. 8—9, 45, no. 1; Grace 1968, p. 175, nos. 2—3; Grace-Savvatianou, pp. 291, 295 note 1, pp. 371, 380.
[188] Nilsson, no. 265; Paris 1914, p. 110, LIII; Porro 1916, p. 117, no. 116; Grace 1934, p. 229, no. 54; Grace 1950, p. 144, no. 70; Pridik, p. 11, nos. 215—223; Levi 1964, p. 265, nos. 116—118; Šelov 1975, nos. 128—132; Gramatopol-Poenaru Bordea, Tomis, p. 57, nos. 51—52; Lazarov 1977, p. 28, no. 66; Calvet 1972, no. 52; Calvet 1978, p. 226, no. 26; Sztetyłło 1984, p. 368, no. 6; Breccia, p. 37, no. 121; Le Roy, p. 242, no. 11; Sztetyłło 1975, p. 183, nos. 80—81; Reisner, p. 313; Macalister, p. 358; Crowfoot, p. 381; Brugnone, pp. 23—24, nos. 33—34; Pellegrini, p. 235, nos. 302—304 and p. 263, nos. 508—510.

53. Inv. no. 16/1976
Villa of Theseus, sector VI/76, upper layer
Diam.: 3 cm
'Επὶ Καλλικρατίδα rose

Stamp of the eponym Kallikratidas II. See no. 51 above.

54. Inv. no. 9/1977
Villa of Theseus, southern wing, surface find
Diam.: 3.2 cm
'Επὶ Καλλικ[ρατί]δα rose

Stamp of the eponym Kallikratidas II. See no. 51 above.

55. Inv. no. 5/1977
Villa of Theseus, southern wing
Dimensions: 3.6 × 1.4 cm
'Επὶ Καλ-
λικρατίδ[α]

Stamp of the eponym Kallikratidas II. See no. 51 above.

56. Inv. no. 13/1978
Villa of Theseus, well SW 80, layer 2
Dimensions: 2.5 × 1.5 cm
'Επὶ Καλ[λικρα-]
τίδα
'Υακινθίου

Stamp of the eponym Kallikratidas II, month Hyakinthios. See no. 51 above.

57. Inv. no. IP/1981
Villa of Theseus, sector VIII/81, above the level of the latitudinal wall
Dimensions: 3.2 × 1.5 cm
Ἐπὶ Κ[αλλικρα-]
τ[ίδα]
Ὑα[κινθίου]

Stamp of the eponym Kallikratidas II, month Hyakinthios. See no. 51 above.

58. Inv. no. IP/1981
Villa of Theseus, sector VI/81, north of the latitudinal wall, below its top
Dimensions: 3.5 × 1.5 cm
Ἐπὶ Κα[λλικρα-]
τί[δα]
Δα[λίου]

Stamp of the eponym Kallikratidas II, month Dalios. See no. 51 above.

59. Inv. no. 15/1983
Villa of Theseus, northern wing, sector 1/82/83, Hellenistic-Roman pottery deposit
Diam.: 3 cm
Circular stamp with a rose in the centre and an inscription around it:
Ἐπὶ Κλεάρχου Ὑακινθίου rose

Stamps of this eponym are missing from the Pergamon group as well as from other well-dated assemblages. The resulting difficulties in dating are increased by the great variety of stamps with the name of Klearchos. In the older literature of the subject it was accepted that Klearchos was eponym sometime in the period 180—150 B.C.[189] Grace, however, is of the opinion that this dating should be moved up, into period II[190]. The variety of stamps is one of Grace's arguments in favour of an earlier dating, for stamps without the title of eponym, which Klearchos also used beside the ones containing this title, appeared on Rhodes in the early stages of stamping. According to Pridik, it cannot

[189] Bleckmann 1912, p. 256, no. 165; Gaertringen, Rhodos, col. 838, no. 186.
[190] Grace 1952, p. 529; Grace 1953, p. 123, no. 106; Grace 1963, p. 326, no. 17; Grace-Savvatianou, p. 293.
[191] See Nachtergael, pp. 25—26, no. 5. See also Pridik 1926, p. 315. Nachtergael, p. 26, is of the opinion that there are historical premises for dating the eponym Klearchos to the second half of the 3rd cent. B.C.
[192] Nilsson, no. 272; Paris 1914, p. 311, LIV; Porro 1916, p. 117, no. 119; Grace 1952, p. 529; Calvet 1978, p. 226, no. 28; Calvet 1982, p. 27, no. 62; Lazarov 1974, p. 48, no. 53; Lazarov 1977, p. 28, no. 67; Breccia, p. 37, no. 124; Empereur 1977, p. 221, no. 64; Nachtergael, no. 5; Crowfoot, p. 381; Sztetyłło 1963, p. 337, no. 4; Sztetyłło 1983, pp. 69—70, nos. 10—12; Sztetyłło 1990, no. 12; Gentili, p. 70, no. 126; Brugnone, p. 24, no. 35; Grace 1956, no. 105; Säflund, p. 14, no. 7. See also Grace 1934, stamps nos. 10950, 11819, 13399.

be excluded that there was a Rhodian producer of this name as well[191].

Stamps with the name of Klearchos are among the most common[192].

60. Inv. no. 7/1988
Late Hellenistic House, upper layer
Dimensions: 3.5 × 1.5 cm
'Επὶ Κλεάρχου
Πανάμου

Stamp of the eponym Klearchos, month Panamos. See no. 59 above.

61. Inv. no. 3/1983
Villa of Theseus, northern wing, sector 13/82/83, upper layer
Dimensions: 4 × 1.5 cm
Rectangular stamp with three lines of inscription:
'Επὶ
Κλευκράτηος
Δαλίου

The presence of the stamps of this eponym in Pergamon permitted a general dating of Kleukrates to the end of the 3rd and beginning of the 2nd cent. B.C.[193] On these grounds Grace considers him an eponym of period III[194]. His dates may be narrowed down to 188—186 B.C. on the basis of the concurrence of small subsidiary stamps introduced in Rhodes around 188 B.C. by the producer Damokrates I[195]. There is a Rhodian amphora found at Olbia that bears the stamps of the eponym Kleukrates and the producer Athanodotos[196]. The latter is known also from stamps found at Pergamon[197]. Another producer who cooperated with Kleukrates was Aristion[198].

Stamps of Kleukrates are not often found in the archaeological material[199].

[193] Schuchhardt, nos. 1087—1096.
[194] Grace 1952, p. 529.
[195] Grace 1985, pp. 8—9. According to Grace, the following eponyms were the first to introduce small subsidiary stamps: Symmachos, Kallikratidas II and Kleukrates, see Grace 1968, p. 175, nos. 2—3; Grace-Savvatianou, p. 291 and 295 note 1, pp. 371, 380. See Šelov 1975, p. 58, no. 134, note 222.
[196] Levi 1964, nos. 120—122.
[197] Schuchhardt, no. 809; Grace 1952, p. 528; Levi 1964, nos. 11—32.
[198] Gentili, pp. 27, 34—35, no. 5.
[199] Nilsson, no. 275; Grace 1956, no. 105; Levi 1964, nos. 120—122; Šelov 1975, no. 134; Lazarov 1977, p. 28, no. 69; Mirčev, no. 99; Calvet 1982, p. 28, no. 63; Crowfoot, p. 381.

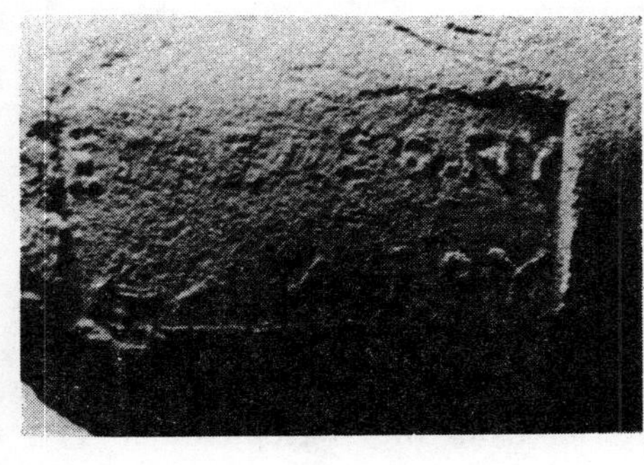

62. Inv. no. 33/1986
Villa of Theseus, room 47 of the southern wing, upper layer
Dimensions: 4×2 cm
Rectangular stamp with three lines of inscription:
'Επὶ Κλεωνύ-
μου
Δαλίου

Among the names recorded on Rhodian amphorae there are two eponyms of the name Kleonymos. Kleonymos I is considered by Grace to be an eponym of the earliest period (I) of stamping amphorae on Rhodes[200]. Kleonymos II is dated to period III in view of the presence of his stamps in Pergamon[201] and in Villanova[202] Our stamp belongs to the latter of the two. Among the Rhodian producers cooperating with Kleonymos II one should mention: Aristos, Damokrates I, Dios, Marsyas and Philon[203].

Stamps of Kleonymos were found on Rhodes, Delos, Cyprus, the Black Sea coast, regions of the ancient Near East and elsewhere[204].

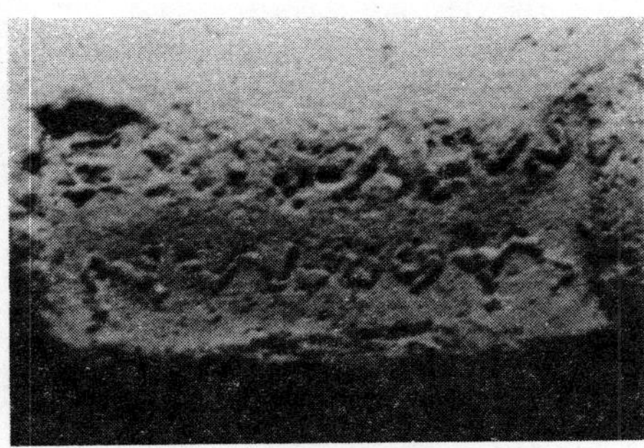

63. Inv. no. 11/1977
Villa of Theseus, western wing
Dimensions: 3.8×1.9 cm
'Επὶ Κλεω-
νύμου

Stamp of the eponym Kleonymos. See no. 62 above.

[200] This group includes the very typical stamps with a "knob" and the name of Hieroteles, see Grace 1963, p. 327 and note 20. The dating of stamps with a "knob" and early names, see Grace-Savatianou, pp. 290, 292, 302, no. E 2, and Grace 1974, p. 200. Two early stamps from Polish excavations, see Sztetyłło 1976, p. 27, no. 1 (Hieroteles) and Sztetyłło 1983, p. 67, no. 4 (Polykrates).

[201] Schuchhardt, nos. 1097—1108.

[202] Maiuri, p. 259, XXXII and p. 262. See also Grace 1952, p. 529; Grace 1953, p. 123, no. 110.

[203] Grace 1934, p. 219; Maiuri, p. 259; Brugnone, p. 26 note 184; Grace, Kyme 1, p. 93; Crowfoot, p. 387; Nicolaou-Empereur, p. 516, no. 2.

[204] Nilsson, no. 277; Paris 1914, p. 311, LVII; Porro 1916, p. 117, no. 122; Grace 1952, p. 529; Levi, Iasos, p. 553, no. 18; Calvet 1972, no. 49; I. Nicolaou, *RDAC* 1965, p. 116, no. 4 d; Sztetyłło 1976, no. 108; Pridik, p. 12, nos. 232—237, and p. 134, nos. 50—51; Canarache, p. 248, no. 579; Lazarov 1974, p. 48, no. 54; Lazarov 1977, p. 28, no. 70; Sztetyłło 1975, p. 190, no. 105; Sztetyłło 1990, no. 27; Reisner, p. 314; Crowfoot, p. 381; Durand, p. 17, no. 43; Börker, p. 38, no. 15; Criscuolo, no. 48; Gentili, p. 72, no. 129; Pellegrini, p. 283, nos. 320—326; Brugnone, p. 26, no. 39.

64. Inv. no. 37/1978
Villa of Theseus, northeastern part
Diam.: 3 cm
'Επὶ Κρατίδα 'Υακινθίου rose

Stamp of the eponym Kratidas, month Hyakinthios. A rose.

This eponym is dated to period III on the basis of finds in Pergamon[205]. His stamps appearing in the well-dated material from the Asclepieion in Pergamon[206], Tarsus[207] and Athens[208] narrowed this down to the end of the 3rd and beginning of the 2nd cent. B.C. The date is corroborated by stamps of producers cooperating with Kratidas, primarily those of Diskos who is well-dated by finds from Villanova[209] and of Agoranax[210], Antigonos[211], Istros[212] and perhaps Philainios[213].

Stamps of Kratidas have been recorded on many archaeological sites[214].

65. Inv. no. IP 1982
Villa of Theseus, surface find
Dimensions: 4.8 × 2 cm
A long rectangular stamp with a legend in three lines:

'Επὶ Νικα-
σ[αγό]ρα
Δαλίου

Of the two Rhodian eponyms of this name, Nikasagoras I has been recorded on stamps from Pergamon[215] and Villanova[216] and this has placed him in period III[217]. Grace narrows this down to 188—183 B.C.[218] The eponym Nikasagoras II was active at a later date as is evidenced by the names of producers appearing on amphorae stamped with his

[205] Schuchhardt, nos. 1112—1119.
[206] Grace 1968, no. 11.
[207] Grace 1950, no. 22.
[208] Grace 1956, no. 102; see also Grace-Savvatianou, p. 294.
[209] Maiuri, p. 254, IX-XVII, p. 254 and 263; Grace, Canaanite, no. 11, pl. XI, nos. 9—11. See also Badal'janc, p. 164.
[210] Badal'janc, p. 163; Grace 1956, nos. 102—103.
[211] Badal'janc, p. 163; Schuchhardt, no. 1119; Bleckmann 1907, p. 22 and 33; Nilsson, p. 105 note 2; Maiuri, p. 254, XIII; Grace, Canaanite, no. 6.
[212] M.B. Wallace, "Some Rhodian Amphora Capacities", *Hesperia* LI, 1982, p. 310.
[213] The combination Kratidas — Philainios is not known.
[214] Nilsson, no. 282; Paris 1914, p. 311, LVIII; Pridik, nos. 242—245; Grace 1950, no. 22; Grace 1952, p. 529; Sztetyłło 1984, no. 7; Calvet 1972, no. 50; Calvet 1982, nos. 64—65; Nachtergael, no. 16; Crowfoot, p. 381; Reisner, p. 314; Macalister, p. 359; Brugnone, no. 40.
[215] Schuchhardt, nos. 1139—1145.
[216] Maiuri, p. 262.
[217] Grace 1952, p. 529.
[218] Grace 1985, p. 8f.

name[219]. Grace places him in period V[220]. Blinkenberg proposes identifying Nikasagoras II with the eponym Nikasagoras Hippokleus who was priest of Athena Lindia in 123 B.C.[221]

The stamp from Paphos should be considered a stamp of Nikasagoras II on the basis of its features. Stamps of this eponym are accompanied sometimes by small subsidiary stamps[222]. His activity should be dated more exactly to the period 146—108 B.C.[223]

Stamps of Nikasagoras, not always correctly distinguished between Nikasagoras I and II, have been recorded in Rhodes, Delos, Tarsus, on the Black Sea coast, regions of the ancient Near East and elsewhere[224].

66. Inv. no. IP/1981

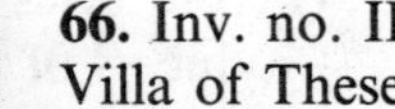

Villa of Theseus, western wing, sector I/81, upper layer

Dimensions: 3.2 × 1.8 cm

['Επὶ Νίκωνος]   bust of Helios

Stamp is badly damaged, reconstruction tentative.

Nikon was one of the Rhodian eponyms of the early period (I) of amphora stamping[225]. Like Hieroteles, Nikon also used so-called stamps with "knobs"[226], permitting a more exact date of his activity to the end of period I or perhaps the beginning of period II (about 240 B.C.)[227]. There are some other stamps of Nikon known, where, beside the eponyms's name, there is a monogram — a characteristic feature of the early period of stamping[228]. Nikon's stamps are as rare in the archaeological record as stamps of the early period in general[229].

[219] These are primarily Agathoboulos and Euphranor from period V, see Nilsson, p. 460, no. 329; Bleckmann 1912, p. 250; Grace-Savvatianou, pp. 305—306, no. E 15; Grace 1965, p. 7, no. 8; Nicolaou-Empereur, p. 351, no. 15. A popular producer of this period, Eukleitos, also cooperated with Nikasagoras II, see Macalister, p. 357, no. 216 and p. 363.

[220] See above, note 120.

[221] Blinkenberg II, I, pp. 24, 125, 536, no. 246. See also Grace 1985, p. 11 note 21.

[222] See above, note 120.

[223] Šelov 1966, p. 666; Grace 1950, no. 76, pl. 117, 76. Nikasagoras I cooperated with several producers, including Damokrates I, Agesippos, Aristokles, Amyntas, Herakleitos and Linos. These producers belonged to the more active ones of the period in question. See Badal'janc, pp. 163—164; Grace-Savvatianou, p. 306, no. E 15; Grace 1985, p. 9 and 45, no. 2; Grace 1950, p. 135 note 2, p. 145, nos. 76—77; Grace 1948, p. 146; Nilsson, p. 118; Maiuri, p. 258, no. 1.

[224] Nilsson, no. 329; Paris 1914, p. 313, LXIV; Porro 1916, p. 119, no. 145; Maiuri, p. 262; Grace 1952, p. 529; Calvet 1972, nos. 72—75; I. Nicolaou, *RDAC* 1970, p. 159, no. 19; Grace 1934, p. 145, no. 76; Pridik, p. 13, nos. 263—269; Levi 1964, p. 266, nos. 123—135; Šelov 1975, nos. 151—154; Lazarov 1977, p. 29, no. 76; Sztetyłło 1975, p. 184, no. 90; Sztetyłło 1990, no. 77; Breccia, p. 41, no. 146; Reisner, p. 313; Macalister, p. 360; Crowfoot, p. 381; Gentili, p. 75, no. 144; Pellegrini, p. 242, nos. 351—354; Brugnone, p. 28, no. 41.

[225] Grace 1952, p. 529; Grace 1934, no. 69.

[226] Nilsson, no. 333 and p. 151; Grace-Savvatianou, p. 290 and 302; Grace 1963, p. 327 and note 20.

[227] Grace 1974, p. 200.

[228] Šelov 1975, no. 157.

[229] Nilsson, no. 333; Porro 1916, no. 148; Grace 1934, no. 69; Grace 1952, p. 529; Calvet 1978, no. 65; Šelov 1975, no. 157; Sztetyłło 1975, nos. 7, 9—10; Sztetyłło 1978, no. 4; Crowfoot, p. 381; Macalister, p. 360; Brugnone, no. 42; Gramatopol-Poenaru Bordea, Dacia XIII, no. 725.

67. Inv. no. 2/1983
Villa of Theseus, northern wing, sector 10/82/83, layer 3
Diam.: 3.2 cm
Round stamp with an olive branch represented in the centre and encircling inscription:
'Επὶ Ξενοφάνευς 'Αρταμιτίου   olive branch

The name of Xenophanes is connected with two Rhodian eponyms. The elder one, Xenophanes I, is attributed to period II[230], the younger — Xenophanes II to period III[231]. Our stamp belongs to the latter. His period of activity is set out by stamps with his name found in Pergamon[232] and Villanova[233]. He is tentatively identified with Xenophanes Hieron, priest of Helios on Rhodes in 189 B.C.[234] Producers of period III known to have cooperated with him according to the evidence of stamps include: Diskos[235], Sokrates[236] and Philainios[237]. Their stamps have been recorded in Pergamon concurrently with the stamps of other eponyms of period III[238].

Stamps of Xenophanes are known from many regions of the ancient world[239].

68. Inv. no. 41/1982
Villa of Theseus, sector 14/82, upper layer
Diam.: 3.7 cm
Circular stamp with an olive branch represented in the centre and encircling inscription:
'Επὶ Ξενοφάνευς   olive branch

Stamp of the eponym Xenophanes II. See no. 67 above.

[230] Grace 1952, p. 529.
[231] Above and Grace-Savvatianou, p. 294 and note 2.
[232] Schuchhardt, nos. 1149—1154.
[233] Maiuri, p. 255 and pp. 256—257, XVIII-XXII.
[234] Brugnone, p. 31.
[235] Maiuri, pp. 255—257, XVIII—XXII. A combination with Diskos is also known from Tarsus, see Grace 1950, p. 140, no. 21 a—b, dated to the beginning of the 2nd cent. B.C. See also Grace 1934, p. 229, no. 56 and p. 219.
[236] Schuchhardt, p. 426; Bleckmann 1907, p. 22 and 31; see also Grace 1934, p. 219 and Badal'janc, p. 165. The name of Sokrates is known also from amphorae stamped by eponyms of period III such as, for example, Hieron I, Ainesidamos, Archidamos, Xenophanes, Sodamos, Sostratos II and Symmachos.
[237] Nilsson, p. 164; Grace 1968, p. 176, no. 9; Grace 1934, p. 219; Badal'janc, p. 165.
[238] The following eponyms are connected with the name of Philainios: Agestratos, Archokrates, Athanadotos, Kratidas, Pratophanes and Timasagoras.
[239] Nilsson, no. 340; Paris 1914, p. 314, LXVIII; Porro 1916, p. 119, no. 152; Grace 1952, p. 529; Calvet 1982, p. 30, no. 74; Sztetyłło 1976, no. 15; Grace 1934, p. 229, no. 56; Grace 1968, pp. 176—177, no. 9; Grace 1950, p. 140, no. 21; Pridik, p. 14, nos. 273—282 and p. 134, nos. 55—60; Šelov 1975, nos. 163—167; Mirčev, nos. 102—103; Lazarov 1974, p. 48, no. 55; Lazarov 1977, p. 29, no. 79; Sztetyłło 1975, p. 186, nos. 92—93; Nachtergael, p. 46; Reisner, p. 313; Macalister, p. 360; Crowfoot, p. 381; Pellegrini, p. 243, nos. 361—363; Brugnone, pp. 30—31, no. 43; Levi, Iasos, p. 555, nos. 24—25.

69. Inv. no. 18/1988
Late Hellenistic House, bottom layer of stone debris fill
Dimensions: 3.5 × 1.7 cm
'Επὶ Ξενο-
φάνευς

Stamp of Xenophanes II. See no. 67 above.

70. Inv. no. 26/1989
Late Hellenistic House, in stone debris layer
Diam.: 3 cm
'Επὶ Ξενοφάντου 'Υακινθίου   rose

Stamp of the eponym Xenophantos, month Hyakinthios.

Most probably there were two eponyms of this name on Rhodes: Xenophantos I active in period II[240] and Xenophantos II active in period IV[241]. Šelov does not exclude a third eponym of this period active in period IV as well[242]. Our stamp belongs to Xenophantos II who cooperated with such known producers of period IV as: Hippokrates son of Damokrates[243], Andrikos[244], Theumnastos[245] and Simias[246]. Xenophantos also used small subsidiary stamps[247] which would suggest that he begun his office after 180 B.C. or put to use from the middle of the century a habit that was becoming more and more popular.

Stamps of Xenophantos are not very common[248].

71. Inv. no. 22/1977
Villa of Theseus, trial pit 69-N/W, layer 5
Diam.: 3.1 cm
'Επὶ Παυσανία Θεσμοφορίου   rose

Stamp of eponym Pausanias, month Thesmophorios.

Of three eponyms of this name Pausanias I is attributed to the beginning of period I[249], Pausanias II to period III[250] and Pausanias III to period IV[251]. Our stamp belongs to Pausanias II who quite

[240] Grace 1952, p. 525; Grace 1934, no. 40.
[241] Grace 1952, p. 525 and 529.
[242] Šelov 1975, pp. 64—65, no. 168.
[243] Badal'janc, p. 164; Grace 1946, pp. 145—146. See also Bleckmann 1907, p. 22 and 32.
[244] Porro, nos. 51—52.
[245] Nilsson, p. 151 — the combination is not confirmed.
[246] Šelov 1975, no. 168 and 451.
[247] Šelov 1975, p. 65; Nilsson, no. 341, 1.
[248] Nilsson, no. 341; Paris 1914, p. 314, LXIX; Grace 1952, p. 525 and 529; Grace 1950, no. 44; Calvet 1978, no. 32; Calvet 1982, nos. 75—77; Levi, Iasos, p. 555, no. 25; Pridik, nos. 283—285; Šelov 1975, no. 168; Mirčev, nos. 104—105; Sztetyłło 1990, no. 31; Crowfoot p. 381; Breccia, p. 41; Gramatopol-Poenaru Bordea, Dacia XIII, no. 1144.
[249] Grace 1953, p. 118 note 3; Grace 1952, p. 529; Grace 1963, p. 324 note 12, p. 326 note 16; Grace-Savvatianou, pp. 297, 304, no. E 12.
[250] See above.
[251] Above and Nachtergael, p. 53, no. 22.

possibly begun functioning at the end of period III and continued his activity into period IV[252]. Evidence in favour of this is supplied by the names of producers who cooperated with him, such as for instance Aristokles and Hippokrates, Imas, Epikrates, Nysios and Hephaistion, and finally Onasioikos[253].

Although not always attributed correctly, stamps of these eponyms are found on many sites[254].

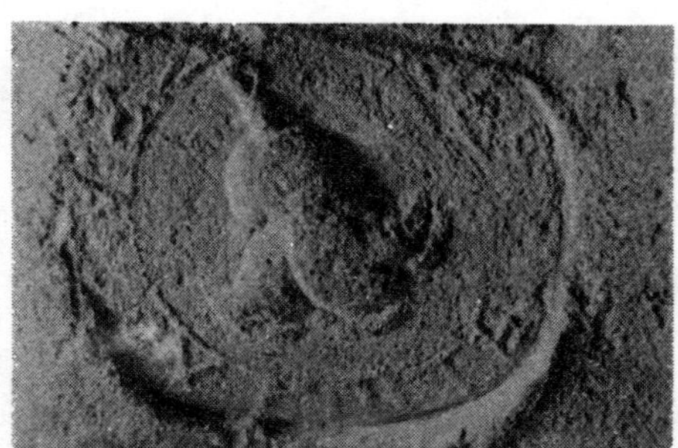

72. Inv. no. 3/1981
Villa of Theseus, sector VI/81, upper layer
Diam.: 3.1 cm

'Ἐπὶ Τεισα[μένου 'Α]γριανίου rose

Stamp of the eponym Teisamenos, month Agrianios.

Grace places this eponym in period V[255]. His period of activity would thus fall in the years 146—108 B.C. He used both rectangular and circular stamps: the circular stamps with the head of Helios, which he also used, are considered by Šelov to be characteristic of the period[256]. Teisamenos cooperated with Midas, a producer known to appear concurrently with the stamps of other eponyms of the third quarter of the 2nd cent. B.C.[257].

Stamps of Teisamenos are not frequent[258].

73. Inv. no. 30/1988
House of Aion, south of room 6, in the fill above the mosaic (ca. 0.70—0.90 m down from the surface)
Dimensions: 4.5×2.2 cm

'Ἐπὶ Τιμασαγόρα
'Αγριανίου

Stamp of the eponym Timasagoras, month Agrianios.

An eponym of period III confirmed by stamps found in the Pergamon deposit[259]; the combination Timasagoras — Aristos was found in Villanova[260].

252 See above.

253 Grace-Savvatianou, no. E 12; Nachtergael, no. 22; Bleckmann 1907, p. 22 and 31; Badal'janc, pp. 164—165; Grace 1934, nos. 4—5; Grace 1952, p. 537, no. 23; Nicolaou-Empereur, no. 7.

254 Nilsson, no. 352; Grace 1952, p. 529; Grace 1934, nos. 36—37; Calvet 1972, nos. 59—60; Calvet 1978, no. 37; Sztetyłło 1976, nos. 122—126; Nicolaou-Empereur, no. 7; Šelov 1975, nos. 173—176; Levi 1964, no. 145; Breccia, p. 42; Empereur 1977, no. 76; Le Roy, no. 12; Sztetyłło 1975, nos. 22—31; Sztetyłło 1983, no. 54; Sztetyłło 1990, no. 55; Crowfoot, p. 382; Börker, no. 1; Brugnone, nos. 45—46, and Gramatopol-Poenaru Bordea, Dacia XIII, nos. 777—780; Mirčev, nos. 105—106.

255 Grace 1952, p. 530.

256 Šelov 1975, p. 72, no. 200.

257 Nicolaou-Empereur, no. 12.

258 Šelov 1975, nos. 200—206; Pridik, no. 398; Sztetyłło 1983, no. 87; Sztetyłło 1975, no. 157; Grace 1952, p. 530; Breccia, p. 45.

259 Schuchhardt, nos. 1194—1203.

260 Maiuri, p. 238, XXIX-XXX, 239 and 262.

He cooperated with many producers of period III: Aristokrates[261], Marsyas[262], possibly Philainios[263] and Philokrates[264]. Šelov is of the opinion that the bust of Helios used as a token by Timasagoras in the left end of his rectangular stamp is characteristic of the end of the 3rd cent. B.C.[265]

Stamps of Timasagoras show a great variety of form and are frequently encountered[266].

74. Inv. no. IP/79
Villa of Theseus, surface find
Dimensions: 3.2 × 1.5 cm
'Επὶ [Τιμασ]αγόρα
Σμινθίου

Stamp of the eponym Timasagoras, month Sminthios. See no. 73.

75. Inv. no. 6/1977
Villa of Theseus, northeastern part of the building
Dimensions: 4 × 1.4 cm
'Επὶ Τιμο-
θέου
'Αγριανίου

Stamp of the eponym Timotheos, month Agrianios.

The eponym is considered by Grace as belonging to period V (ca 146—108 B.C.)[267] or to period IV (ca 175—146 B.C.)[268]. Timotheos also used small subsidiary stamps which became especially common in the second half of the 2nd cent. B.C. [268]. Stamps of Timotheos are found in Nea Paphos[270], Lindos[271], Tanais[272], but are not frequent[273].

[261] Badal'janc, p. 164; Calvet 1972, nos. 38, 51.
[262] Gentili, p. 28.
[263] Schuchhardt, no. 1197; Börker, p. 44 note 91.
[264] Badal'janc, p. 165; Nilsson, p. 76.
[265] Šelov 1975, pp. 73—74, no. 209.
[266] Nilsson, no. 406; Paris, p. 316, LXXXVI; Grace 1952, p. 530; Pridik, nos. 369—377; Šelov 1975, nos. 209—211; Levi 1964, nos. 158—159; Gramatopol-Poenaru Bordea, Dacia XIII, no. 730; Calvet 1982, nos. 91—92; Calvet 1972, nos. 38, 51; Sztetyłło 1976, no. 133(?); Crowfoot, p. 382; Macalister, p. 362; Reisner, p. 315; Empereur 1977, nos. 85—86; Brugnone, no. 55.
[267] Grace 1952, p. 530.
[268] Grace 1950, p. 143, no. 47.
[269] Crowfoot, p. 315, no. 9.
[270] Sztetyłło 1976, p. 70, no. 215
[271] Nilsson, no. 411.
[272] Šelov 1975, nos. 214—215.
[273] See above, notes 267—272.

76. Inv. no. 10/1987
Late Hellenistic House, southwestern part, ca 15 cm above mosaic level, between blocks of the wall in sector 3/87
Part of a rectangular stamp, preserved dimensions: 2.5 × 1.5 cm
The front parts of three lines have been preserved:
'Επὶ ἱ[ερέως]
Τιμ[ουρρόδου]
[Π]αν[άμου]

Assuming the reconstruction is correct, the stamp gives the name of Timourrodos preceded by the title of eponym; the name of the month is Panamos.

Grace places this eponym in period IV, thus he would fall in the years 175—146 B.C.[274] Such a dating is confirmed by the absence of stamps of this eponym from the Pergamon deposit and from other well-dated groups of stamps from the end of the 3rd and the first half of the 2nd cent. B.C.[275] It appears to be corroborated further by the eponym's use of small subsidiary stamps which were introduced only about 188 B.C. and became especially widespread in the second half of the 2nd cent. B.C.[276] Timourrodos cooperated with such producers of this period as Imas and Hermias (especially Imas known from many stamps) who in their turn are confirmed by appearing on amphorae concurrently with other eponyms of period IV[277].

Stamps of Timourrodos have been recorded on many sites[278].

77. Inv. no. 14/1984
Villa of Theseus, northwestern corner of the building
Dimensions: 4 × 1.8 cm
Rectangular stamp with two lines of inscription:
'Επὶ Φιλοδάμου
Θεσμοφορίου

The eponym Philodamos is placed by Grace among eponyms of period III[279]. He may be dated more precisely thanks to his stamps appearing

[274] Grace 1952, p. 530; See also Grace-Savvatianou, p. 305, no. E 14.
[275] Grace 1950, p. 143, no. 48. See also Bleckmann 1912, p. 258, no. 242, and Gaertringen, Rhodos, no. 292.
[276] Grace-Savvatianou, p. 305, no. E 14.
[277] Imas cooperated with the eponyms: Autokrates, Damainetos, Pausanias III and Pythodoros. See Grace, Amphoras, fig. 31; Grace-Savvatianou, p. 304, no. E 7; Badal'janc, p. 165 (Autokrates). Graces dates Damainetos to before 150 B.C., see Grace-Savvatianou, pp. 303—304, no. E 7. The combination Imas-Damainetos, see Grace, Amphoras, fig. 31; Badal'janc, p. 165; Nilsson, p. 115; Grace 1934, p. 219. The combination Imas — Pausanias III, see Grace 1953, p. 118 and note 5; Grace 1934, p. 219; Bleckmann 1907, p. 22 and 32; Schuchhardt, p. 425; Porro, p. 382, nos. 13—14; Badal'janc, p. 165.
The combination Imas — Pythodoros, see Porro, p. 382, nos. 15—16.
[278] Nilsson, no. 416; Grace 1952, p. 530; Grace-Savvatianou, p. 305, no. E 14; Grace 1950, p. 143, no. 48; Pridik, p. 19; Šelov 1975, nos. 223—226; Sztetyłło 1975, no. 109; Sztetyłło 1976, nos. 162—165; Sztetyłło 1983, nos. 68—69; Sztetyłło 1990, no. 57; Crowfoot, p. 382.
[279] Grace 1952, p. 530; Grace 1953, p. 124, no. 168; Grace 1934, p. 226, no. 43; Grace 1968, p. 176.

concurrently with the stamps of the most active producer of the period, Damokrates I[280]. Among other cooperating producers one should mention Aristos[281] and Philainios[282].

Stamps with the name of the eponym Philodamos were found in Rhodes, Delos, Cyprus, Athens, Tarsus to list some[283].

78. Inv. no. 5/1985
Villa of Theseus, western wing, sector 1/85, upper layer
Diam.: 3 cm
Circular stamp with a representation of a rose and encircling inscription:

Ἐπὶ Φιλοδάμου Θεσμοφορίου rose

Stamp of the eponym Philodamos. See no. 77 above.

PRODUCERS

79. Inv. no. 4/1987
Late Hellenistic House, south of room 48B, sector 1/87, layer II (debris of fallen wall, destroyed in an earthquake)
Dimensions: 3.5 × 1.5 cm
Rectangular stamp with one line of legend. Stars in the upper corners of the stamp, an unclear representation in the lower right corner: a flower? torch?

Ἀγαθοκλ (εῦς) stars

Of the two Rhodian producers bearing the same name[284] Agathokles II, to whom our stamp should be attributed, is dated by finds from Pergamon[285] and by the concurrent stamps of eponyms Agestratos II[286], Athanodotos[287] and Symmachos[288]. On this basis it is possible to place his activity more

[280] Grace 1950, p. 135, no. 2 and p. 145, nos. 72—73. See also Badal'janc, p. 164.
[281] Maiuri, p. 259, XXXI; Bleckmann 1907, pp. 22—23; Badal'janc, p. 165.
[282] Hall, p. 392, 5049. For a discussion of the identification of the eponym Philodamos and his dating see Nachtergael, pp. 44—46, no. 17.
[283] Schuchhardt, nos. 1213—1220; Maiuri, p. 259, XXXI; Nilsson, p. 424; Grace 1952, p. 530; Sztetyłło 1976, p. 53, no. 137; Levi, Iasos, p. 557, no. 35; Grace 1950, p. 141, nos. 24b—25; Grace 1934, p. 226, no. 43; Canarache, no. 529; Lazarov 1977, p. 31, no. 108; Lazarov 1974, p. 44, no. 63; I. Nicolaou, *RDAC* 1965, p. 115, no. 4 f; Breccia, p. 46, no. 192; Sztetyłło 1975, no. 98; Nachtergael, pp. 44—46, no. 17; Reisner, p. 315; Crowfoot, p. 382; Gentili, p. 185.
[284] Grace 1985, p. 10.
[285] Schuchhardt, nos. 766—774.
[286] Bleckmann 1907, pp. 22 and 31; Badal'janc, p. 163.
[287] Grace 1949, no. 23; Grace 1985, p. 10.
[288] Gentili, no. 20a—b.

precisely in the end of the 3rd cent. B.C.

Stamps of Agathokles are to be found on many archaeological sites[289].

80. Inv. no. 20/1975
Villa of Theseus, surface find
Dimensions: 4 × 1.6 cm
['Αγαθοκ]λεῦς

Stamp of the producer Agathokles. See no. 79 above.

81. Inv. no. 10/1978
Villa of Theseus, well SW 80
Dimensions: 4.1 × 1.6 cm
'Αγάθων

There is little to determine the chronological range of the producer Agathon. The form of the handle, of the stamp itself and of the letters suggests the second half of the 2nd cent. B.C., cf. Sztetyłło 1984, no. 16; Gramatopol-Poenaru Bordea, Dacia XIII, nos. 742—743.

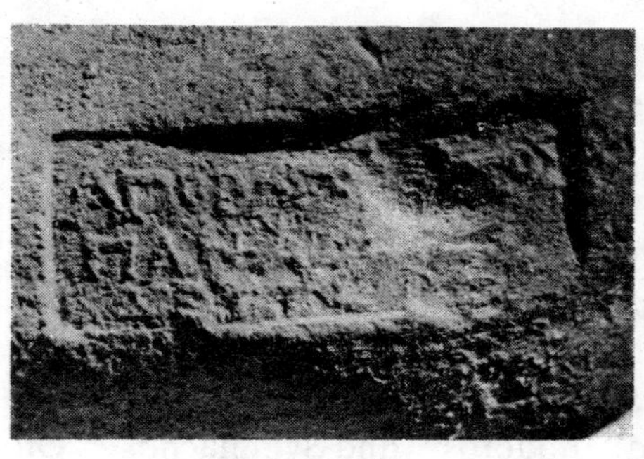

82. Inv. no. 23/1983
House of Aion, room 3, above mosaic floor level
Dimensions: 3.7 × 1.5 cm
Rectangular stamp with three lines of inscription:
'Αγοράν[ακ]τος
Πανάμου
δευτέρου

Stamps with the name of the producer Agoranax were found in Pergamon and Villanova[290]. The general dating to the end of the 3rd and beginning of the 2nd cent. B.C. was narrowed down by Grace to 221—199 B.C.; it covers both the end of period II

[289] Nilsson, no. 7; Paris 1914, p. 301; Porro 1916, p. 109, no. 1; Grace 1952, p. 525; Calvet 1972, p. 25, no. 39; Calvet 1978, p. 223, no. 1; Calvet 1982, p. 16, nos. 12—14; Sztetyłło 1976, p. 31, no. 22; Grace 1934, p. 228, no. 51; Grace 1950, p. 141, no. 35; Pridik, p. 21, nos. 423—438; Levi 1964, p. 267, nos. 160—169; Šelov 1975, nos. 254—258; Mirčev, no. 120; Lazarov 1974, p. 44, no. 68; Lazarov 1977, p. 33, no. 1; Gramatopol-Poenaru Bordea, Tomis, p. 58, no. 61; Gramatopol-Poenaru Bordea, Dacia XIII, p. 264, nos. 1145, 1175; Breccia, p. 20, no. 1; Criscuolo, no. 74; Sztetyłło 1975, p. 172, nos. 35—36; Reisner, p. 311; Sztetyłło 1983, p. 71, no. 14; Macalister, p. 351; Crowfoot, p. 382; Dunand II, 2, p. 799, no. 15754; Börker, p. 42, no. 27; Pellegrini, p. 197, nos. 1—14; Brugnone, p. 43, no. 60; Benoit, p. 30, no. 6; Säflund, p. 13, no. 1.

[290] Schuchhardt, nos. 804—808; Maiuri, p. 260.

and the beginning of period III[291]. Other eponyms of period II whose stamps accompanied those of Agoranax include Tharsipolis[292] and Sostratos[293]; Aratophanes[294] and Kratidas[295] belonged to eponyms of period III.

Stamps of Agoranax, containing also the name of the month, are frequently encountered in the archaeological record[296].

83. Inv. no. 27/1977
Villa of Theseus, sector W/80/77
Dimensions: 3.4 × 1.3 cm
Ἀγορ[άνα]κτος
Πανάμου
δευτέρου

Stamp of producer Agoranax. See no. 82 above.

84. Inv. no. 21/1977
Villa of Theseus, trial pit 69-N/W, layer 5
Diam.: 3 cm
Αἰνέα

Stamp of producer Aineas, dated in general terms to period III (ca 210—175 B.C.) on the basis of the Pergamon deposit finds[297]. This producer may have cooperated with the eponym Thestor[298]; in such a case the date would be narrowed down to the end of the 3rd cent. B.C. Šelov emphasizes the token used by Aineas — a wreath; the same token was used by other producers of the end of the 3rd and beginning of the 2nd cent. B.C., namely Amyntas and Philainios to give but two examples[299].

Stamps of Aineas are not very common[300].

[291] Grace 1974, p. 200. See also Grace-Savvatianou, p. 302, no. E 1.

[292] Crowfoot, p. 387.

[293] Grace 1956, p. 143, no. 102; Grace, Amphoras, fig. 25; Grace-Savvatianou, no. E 1 and E 5; Badal'janc, p. 163.

[294] Bleckmann 1907, p. 32; Bleckmann 1912, p. 251; Grace 1934, p. 219; Porro 1916, p. 108; Badal'janc, p. 163. Grace dates Aratophanes to around 181 B.C., see Grace 1985, p. 8.

[295] Grace 1956, pp. 143—144, nos. 102—103; Grace, Amphoras, fig. 25; Grace-Savvatianou, p. 302, no. E 1; Badal'janc, p. 163.

[296] Nilsson, no. 19; Paris, p. 156, VIII; Paris 1914, p. 302, V; Porro 1916, p. 109, no. 8; Grace 1952, p. 525; Grace-Savvatianou, p. 302, no. E 1; Calvet 1972, no. 36; I. Nicolaou, *RDAC* 1968, p. 94, no. 24; Sztetyłło 1976, nos. 3—5; Calvet 1982, p. 17, nos. 16—18; Grace 1934, p. 228, nos. 49—50; Grace 1956, p. 144, no. 103; Pridik, p. 21, nos. 443—450; Levi 1964, p. 267, nos. 173—174; Lazarov 1974, p. 49, nos. 69—70; Lazarov 1977, p. 33, no. 4; Breccia, p. 20, no. 5; Empereur 1977, pp. 204—205, nos. 7—10; Sztetyłło 1975; no. 41; Sztetyłło 1978, no. 15; Sztetyłło 1983, nos. 17—20; Reisner, p. 312; Macalister, p. 352; Crowfoot, p. 382; Börker, p. 35, no. 4; Criscuolo, nos. 75—76; Gentili, p. 41; Pellegrini, p. 200, nos. 30—40; Brugnone, p. 46, nos. 64—65; Säflund, p. 13, no. 3.

[297] Schuchhardt, nos. 822—826.

[298] Grace, Kyme 1, p. 193.

[299] Šelov 1975, no. 260.

[300] Nilsson, no. 28; Paris 1914, p. 302, VII; Pridik, no. 453; Šelov 1975, nos. 260—261; Sztetyłło 1976, no. 218; Crowfoot, p. 382.

85. Inv. no. 35/1987
House of Aion, foundation trench northwest of room 1
Dimensions: 3 × 1.5 cm
Rectangular stamp with a one-line inscription and a representation of a herm lying sideways to the left of the inscription.
'Αμύντα herm

Amyntas was one of the more active Rhodian producers of period III if we are to judge by the number of stamps found on many sites. The presence of his stamps in the Pergamon deposit placed him in period III, that is at the beginning of the 2nd cent. B.C.[301] He cooperated with eponyms attributed to both period III and period IV such as Athanodotos[302], Archilaidas[303], Aristomachos[304], Xenophon[305] and Symmachos[306] and this narrows down his dating to the years 191—176 B.C.[307]

A characteristic feature of the stamps of Amyntas is the herm or wreath beside his name. The herm, very finely executed at times, may have been inspired by a sculptured herm[308].

As mentioned above already, stamps of Amyntas are encountered on numerous archaeological sites[309].

86a

86. Inv. no. 24/1976
Villa of Theseus, sector I/76
Diam.: 3.1 cm
'Αναξιππίδα rose

Stamp of Anaxippidas.

Data on the activities of Anaxippidas is missing. There were no stamps of his in the Pergamon deposit suggesting a later dating and there are no

[301] Schuchhardt, nos. 856—859.
[302] Grace 1950, p. 135 note 2 and p. 141, nos. 29—30. See also Grace 1985, p. 10 and note 19, and p. 9; Nicolaou-Empereur, p. 517, no. 3.
[303] Šelov 1975, no. 264, and no. 78.
[304] Gentili, no. 18.
[305] Bleckmann 1907, p. 33; Hall, p. 390, no. 5066; Badal'janc, p. 163; Grace 1948, p. 145.
[306] Gentili, no. 11.
[307] Grace 1985, p. 10.
[308] Z. Sztetyłło, "Les hermes dans l'iconographie des timbres amphoriques grecs", *EtTrav* 5, 1971, pp. 91—103, suggests that the Dionysiac herm of Boethos may have been the model for some of the representations of herms on Rhodian stamps, including the stamps of Amyntas. Nachtergael discusses this hypothesis on pp. 29—30.
[309] Nilsson, no. 42; Grace 1952, p. 526; Paris, p. 157, XI; Porro, p. 112; Pridik, p. 22; Šelov 1975, p. 83, nos. 263—264; Levi 1964, nos. 185—193; Grace 1950, p. 141, no. 30; Calvet 1982, p. 17, no. 21; Sztetyłło 1976, nos. 33—40; Breccia, p. 22, no. 18; Nachtergael, p. 27, no. 6; Börker, no. 23 and 30; Macalister, p. 533; Crowfoot, p. 382; Sztetyłło 1975, no. 223.

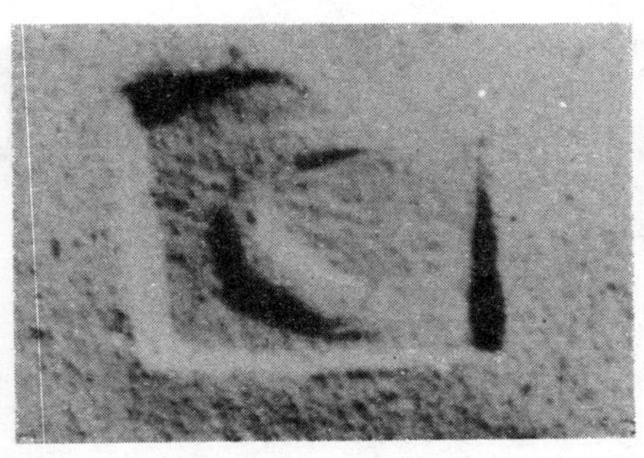

86b

combinations with names of eponyms, disregarding the one debatable concurrence of Anaxippidas' name with that of the eponym Leontidas[310]. Presumably, he belongs to the middle of the 2nd cent. B.C., a period which is also suggested by the use of subsidiary stamps[311].

These stamps are rare in the archaeological record[312].

87. Inv. no. IP 1982
Villa of Theseus, surface find from the southern part of the residence
Dimensions: 4×1.8 cm
A long rectangular stamp with one line of inscription and a representation of a caduceus lying horizontally to the right, below the legend.
'Αντιμάχου

A rectangular stamp with the caduceus shown horizontally is characteristic of Antimachos. His stamps in the Pergamon deposit define his period of activity[313]. It must have reached beyond the year 175 B.C. for there appear on amphorae concurrently with his stamps the stamps of such eponyms as: Athanodotos[314], Aleximachos[315], Hieron I[316] and Pratophanes[317].

Stamps of Antimachos are profusely represented in the material from various sites[318].

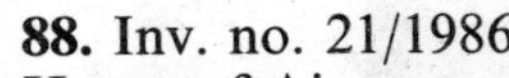

88. Inv. no. 21/1986
House of Aion, room 3, layer 4
Dimensions: 4×1.7 cm
Rectangular stamp with one line of inscription and stars in the corners.
'Αριστάρχου stars

A kind of stamp that is characteristic for the producer Aristarchos. The name was recorded among the Pergamon finds[319]. Aristarchos coope-

310 Šelov 1975, no. 265 and notes 405—406.
311 Šelov 1956, p. 139, no. 51.
312 Nilsson, no. 48; Pridik, no. 472; Šelov 1975, nos. 265—266; Sztetyłło 1990, no. 60; Säflund, no. 17; Crowfoot, p. 382.
313 Schuchhardt, nos. 861—864.
314 The name of Athanodotos was discovered on stamps from Pergamon, see Schuchhardt, nos. 809—811. Grace dates his activity to the years 188—183 B.C., see Grace 1985, p. 8. For the combination Athanodotos — Antimachos, see Schuchhardt, p. 425 and Badal'janc, p. 164.
315 Pridik 1926, p. 321 and 331; Badal'janc, p. 163. See also Grace 1950, p. 136 and 142, nos. 39—40 (stamps of Aleximachos and his dating to the second quarter of the 2nd cent. B.C.).
316 Gentili, pp. 27, 29, 67, no. 120. Grace places Hieron at the beginning of the 2nd cent. B.C. See Grace 1950, pp. 136, 144, no. 71, and Grace 1985, p. 23 note 60.
317 Badal'janc, p. 164.
318 Nilsson, no. 55; Paris 1914, p. 303, XI; Grace 1952, p. 526; Sztetyłło 1976, p. 37, no. 50; Pridik, p. 22, no. 491; Levi 1964, p. 268, nos. 195—207; Šelov 1975, nos. 271—275; Lazarov 1977, p. 34, no. 7; Breccia, no. 26; Börker, p. 37, no. 11, p. 42, no. 29; Sztetyłło 1983, no. 25; Crowfoot, p. 382.
319 Schuchhardt, nos. 875—877.

rated with eponyms of period III, Ainetor[320] and Symmachos[321].

His stamps are often encountered in the material and have been recorded in Rhodes, Delos, Cyprus, regions of the ancient Near East and on the Black Sea coast[322].

89. Inv. no. 4/1983
Villa of Theseus, northern wing, sector 4/83
Dimensions: 4 × 1.7 cm
Rectangular stamp with one line of inscription and stars in the corners.

'Αρισ[τά]ρχου stars

Stamp of the producer Aristarchos. See no. 88 above.

90. Inv. no. 45/1986
Villa of Theseus, northern wing, sector 1 B/86, below wall with preserved murals
Dimensions: 3.2 × 1.7 cm
Rectangular stamp with one line of inscription and stars in the corners.

'Αριστάρχου stars

Stamp of Aristarchos. See no. 88 above.

91. Inv. no. 6/1987
Late Hellenistic House, sector 1/87, layer II (below the upper layer consisting of the debris of the northern wall)
Dimensions: 3.5 × 1.5 cm
Rectangular stamp with one line of inscription and stars in the corners and a representation of the sun below the legend.

'Αριστάρχου stars and the sun

Stamp of Aristarchos. See no. 88 above.

[320] For the amphora from Monte Iudica see Brugnone, no. 66.

[321] For the amphora from Syracuse see Gentili, p. 35, nos. 9—10 and no. 20. Grace dates the activity of Symmachos to the years 188—186 B.C. thanks to the concurrence of this eponym's stamps with the stamps of the producer Damokrates I. See Grace 1968, p. 175, no. 3; Grace-Savvatianou, pp. 291, 295 note 1, 371; Grace 1985, p. 8 and 45, no. 1.

[322] Nilsson, no. 79; Paris 1914, p. 303, XII; Porro 1916, p. 112, no. 25; Grace 1952, p. 526; Sztetyłło 1976, no. 53 and 238; Breccia, p. 25, no. 35; Sztetyłło 1975, p. 174, nos. 44—45; Reisner, p. 311; Macalister, p. 354; Crowfoot, p. 382; Pridik, p. 23, nos. 507—510, p. 135, no. 85; Levi 1964, p. 268, nos. 209—211; Šelov 1975, no. 285; Lazarov 1977, p. 34, no. 11; Mirčev, no. 122; Gramatopol-Poenaru Bordea, Tomis, p. 58, no. 63; Gramatopol-Poenaru Bordea, Dacia XIII, p. 233, no. 741; Gentili, p. 46, no. 48; Pellegrini, p. 210, nos. 107—109; Brugnone, pp. 47—48, no. 68; Levi, Iasos, p. 549, no. 4.

92. Inv. no. 22/1986
House of Aion, room 3, layer 3 (ca 0.95—1.65 m down from the surface)
Dimensions: 3.5 × 1.5 cm
Part of a rectangular stamp with two lines of inscription:
Δαλίου
'Αριστείδα

Stamps of Aristeidas found in Pergamon form the chronological frame for his activity[323]. Upon analysis of the concurring official stamps, it may be assumed that Aristeidas worked in the end of period II continuing through the beginning of period III[324]. One of the eponyms who cooperated with Aristeidas was Thestor[325].

Stamps of Aristeidas are not very widespread[326].

93. Inv. no. IP/1984
Villa of Theseus, northern wing, upper layer
Diam.: 3 cm
Circular stamp with a representation of a rose and encircling legend:
'Αριστοκλεῦς rose

Aristokles was one of the more active Rhodian producers of the first quarter of the 2nd cent. B.C. and his stamps have been found on many sites including Pergamon[327]. His stamps are accompanied by the stamps of eponyms belonging to periods III and IV, that is from the beginning of the 2nd cent. B.C.: Archilaidas[328], Nikasagoras I[329], Pausanias[330], Aratophanes I[331] and Ariston[332]. Aristokles was one of those producers who stamped amphorae on Cuidos as well[333] and who used small subsidiary stamps[334].

Stamps of Aristokles are very common and appear on many sites[335].

[323] Schuchhardt, nos. 887—890.

[324] In favour of this thesis is the fact that Aristeidas used representations of stars on his stamps. This representation appears on the stamps of some eponyms of the end of period II and beginning of period III. See Nilsson, p. 155 and 159; Paris, p. 172.

[325] Paris, p. 172; Badal'janc, p. 164; Börker, p. 35, no. 6. Thestor's stamps were found at Pergamon, see Schuchhardt, nos. 1032—1035, while he is assigned by Grace to the last quarter of the 3rd cent. B.C., see Grace-Savvatianou, p. 294, and Grace 1963, p. 325 and 334, no. 9 and fig. 1, 9 on p. 323; Grace, Amphoras, fig. 22.

[326] Nilsson, no. 81; Paris 1914, p. 304, XIII; Porro 1916, p. 112, no. 26; Grace 1952, p. 526; Calvet 1978, p. 224, no. 9; Grace 1934, p. 230, no. 57; Pridik, p. 23, nos. 511—515; Mirčev, no. 123; Lazarov 1977, p. 34, no. 12; Gramatopol-Poenaru Bordea, Dacia XIII, p. 230, no. 709; Breccia, p. 25, no. 36; Reisner, p. 313; Börker, p. 35, no. 6; Sztetyłło 1975, no. 47; Gentili, p. 46, no. 49; Pellegrini, p. 211, nos. 113—114; Brugnone, p. 48, no. 67.

[327] Schuchhardt, nos. 916—917. See also Grace 1985, p. 10 and 18.

[328] For the combination Aristokles — Archilaidas see Pridik, p. 23, no. 523, and Šelov 1975, p. 88, no. 288; Grace 1949, p. 187, pl. 19, 5, and 20, 4, 5; Grace-Savvatianou, p. 279 note 2 and p. 291 note 3; Grace 1985, pp. 11, 17 and 23 note 61; Badal'janc, p. 164; Nicolaou-Empereur, p. 519, no. 5.

[329] Grace 1950, p. 135 note 2 and p. 145, nos. 76—77.

[330] Badal'janc, p. 164.

[331] Grace 1934, p. 219; Grace 1949, p. 174 and 189, nos. 4—5; Grace-Savvatianou, p. 313, no. E 34.

[332] As above and Breccia, p. 27; Nicolaou-Empereur, p. 519, no. 5. Badal'janc, p. 164, also mentions the combinations Aristokles — the eponym Eudamos, and Aristokles — the eponym Timodikos.

94. Inv. no. 20/1983
Villa of Theseus, northeastern part of the building, sector 5/82/83
Dimensions: 4.3 × 1.8 cm
Rectangular stamp with one line of inscription and a caduceus represented horizontally to the right below the legend.
'Αρίστωνος caduceus

The name of the producer Ariston was confirmed in the Pergamon deposit[336]. He should probably be dated to the beginning of the 2nd cent. B.C. because his stamps appear together with stamps bearing the names of eponyms from the period 188—183 B.C., including Agemachos[337] and Athanodotos[338].

Stamps of Ariston are found exceptionally often on the shores of the Black Sea[339].

95. Inv. no. 8/1987
Late Hellenistic House, southwestern part of the excavation, south of room 29, ca 15 cm above floor level, in between the blocks of the structure destroyed by a quake
Dimensions: 3.3 × 1.5 cm
Partly damaged rectangular stamp with one line of inscription. Beginning of name destroyed. A caduceus(?) below.
['Αρίσ]τωνος caduceus(?)

Stamp of Ariston. See no. 94 above.

96. Inv. no. 13/1988
Late Hellenistic House, in the stone debris above the stylobate of the portico
Dimensions: 4 × 2 cm
'Αρίστωνος caduceus to the right

Stamp of the producer Ariston. See no. 94 above.

[333] Grace-Savvatianou, pp. 327—328, nos. E 66 - E 68 and pp. 280, 320.
[334] Šelov 1975, p. 89 and note 450; Šelov 1966, p. 666.
[335] Nilsson, no. 100; Paris, p. 158, XXII; Grace 1952, p. 526; Calvet 1982, p. 20, no. 32; Sztetyłło 1976, p. 28, nos. 54—55; Sztetyłło 1984, no. 10; Lenger 1957, p. 164, no. 88; Levi, Iasos, p. 549, no. 7; Grace 1950, p. 145, nos. 77—78; Pridik, p. 23, no. 523; Levi 1964, nos. 216—219; Šelov 1975, p. 88, no. 288; Lazarov 1974, p. 49, no. 71; Lazarov 1977, p. 34, no. 16; Sztetyłło 1983, p. 78, no. 31; Breccia, p. 26; Sztetyłło 1975, p. 176, nos. 52—53; Sztetyłło 1990, no. 18; Börker, p. 43, no. 33; Crowfoot, p. 382; Empereur 1977, pp. 207—208, nos. 17—18; Säflund, p. 19, no. 18.
[336] Schuchhardt, nos. 936—941; see also Bleckmann 1907, p. 31 and Bleckmann 1912, p. 252.
[337] Bleckmann 1907 and 1912, loc. cit.; Badal'janc, p. 164; Nachtergael, p. 36, no. 11, note 10.
[338] Grace 1985, p. 10. See also Paris 1914, p. 326, with the eponym Dorchylidas.
[339] Nilsson, no. 114; Levi 1964, nos. 222—223; Pridik, p. 110, nos. 182—185; Mirčev, p. 32, no. 127; Lazarov 1977, p. 35, no. 20; Canarache, no. 620; Paris 1914, p. 304, XV; Breccia, p. 27; Le Roy, BIFAO 84, p. 310, nos. 9—10; Levi, Iasos, p. 549, no. 5; Crowfoot, p. 382.

97. Inv. no. 2/1981
Villa of Theseus, western wing, sector V/81, below the top of the latitudinal wall
Dimensions: 4 × 1.8 cm
'Αριστίωνος

Stamp of the producer Aristion. The name was registered among the Pergamon finds[340] and it is known from amphorae bearing also the names of the eponyms: Dorchylidas[341], Kleitomachos[342] and Kleukrates[343]. In conformity with this, Aristion's activity should be dated to the end of the 3rd and beginning of 2nd cent. B.C.[344]

Aristion's stamps are often encountered[345].

98. Inv. no. 7/1979
Villa of Theseus, room 86, upper layer
Dimensions: 4 × 1.8 cm
'Αριστίωνος

Stamp of the producer Aristion. See no. 97 above.

99. Inv. no. IP 1979
Found near the Villa of Theseus.
Dimensions: 4 × 1.8 cm
['Αριστί]ωνος

Stamp of the producer Aristion. See no. 97 above.

[340] Schuchhardt, nos. 891—892.
[341] Badal'janc, p. 164; Paris, p. 334; Grace 1985, p. 40.
[342] Grace 1985, p. 40.
[343] Gentili, no. 6.
[344] Grace 1985, p. 40, p. 8.
[345] Nilsson, no. 85; Paris 1914, p. 304, XV; Grace 1934, no. 46; Grace 1952, p. 526; Grace 1950, nos. 17—18; Calvet 1972, nos. 25—28; Sztetyłło 1976, nos. 56—58; Calvet 1982, nos. 28—30; Pridik, nos. 516—520; Šelov 1975, nos. 286—287; Sztetyłło 1975, nos. 49—51; Sztetyłło 1983, no. 29; Le Roy, BIFAO 84, nos. 9—10; Crowfoot, p. 382; Reisner, p. 311; Macalister, p. 354; Brugnone, nos. 68—70; Levi, Iasos, p. 549, no. 5; Gramatopol-Poenaru Bordea, Dacia XIII, no. 749; Mirčev, nos. 124—125.

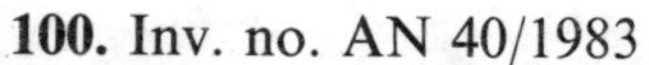

100. Inv. no. AN 40/1983
Villa of Theseus, sector 5/82/83 (Hellenistic levels)
Dimensions: 2.5 × 1.8 cm
Rectangular stamp with a two-line inscription preserved fragmentarily.

'Αρτεμί-
δωρος

This is presumably a stamp of the producer Artemidoros whose name is known from the Pergamon deposit[346]. The most common form of this producer's stamp is, as in our case, a rectangular field containing an inscription in two lines with his name and the name of the month.

The stamps of this producer are not very frequent[347].

101. Inv. no. IP/1981
Villa of Theseus, from the baulk between sectors V and VI, below the top edge of wall N-S
Dimensions: 4 × 2 cm

Βρομίου

Stamp of the producer Bromios. Since his stamps were missing from the Pergamon deposit, it was considered that this producer was active at a later time. Grace first placed him in the period ca 180—150 B.C.[349], but later discovered combinations with stamps of eponyms: Alexiadas[349], Autokrates[350], Gorgon[351] and Pythodoros[352], setting a firm date for this producer in the end of period IV and beginning of period V.

Stamps of Bromios with the characteristic token in the form of a wreath are frequent[353].

102. Inv. no. IP/1981
Surface find from the vicinity of the Villa of Theseus
Dimensions: 4.1 × 1.8 cm

Γλαυκία

Stamp of the producer Glaukias. His is a rare stamp with only four being recorded by Nilsson[354]. The combination Glaukias — eponym Klenostratos[355], places him in the second half of the 2nd cent. B.C.[356]

I have already emphasized that this is a rare stamp[357].

[346] Schuchhardt, no. 943. There may have existed an earlier homonym, see Grace 1934, nos. 26—27 and Grace 1956, p. 142, no. 82.

[347] Nilsson, no. 122; Grace 1934, nos. 26—27; Empereur 1977, no. 22; Mirčev, no. 129; Šelov 1975, no. 293; Grace 1956, p. 142, no. 82; Crowfoot, p. 382.

[348] Grace 1934, no. 60; Grace 1950, nos. 51—53.

[349] Brugnone, p. 70 note 392.

[350] Börker, no. 85.

[351] Brugnone, p. 70 note 389.

[352] Börker, nos. 34—35.

[353] Nilsson, no. 146; Paris 1914, p. 307, XXIV; Grace 1952, p. 526; Grace 1950, nos. 51—53; Sztetyłło 1976, nos. 151—152; Pridik, nos. 548—554; Šelov 1975, no. 302; Breccia, p. 30; Sztetyłło 1975, no. 101; Sztetyłło 1983, nos. 60—61; Sztetyłło 1990, no. 39; Empereur 1977, no. 27; Crowfoot, p. 383; Reisner, p. 311; Brugnone, no. 77.

[354] Nilsson, no. 149.

103. Inv. no. 36/1987
Late Hellenistic House, sector 13/87, upper layer
Dimensions: 5×3 cm
Rectangular stamp badly damaged. Of the presumably two-line inscription only the first letter has been preserved and a representation of a pilos with a star in the second one.

Δ[αματρίου] pilos and star

There were two among the Rhodian producers who employed representation of a pilos and a star on their stamps — Damatrios[358] and Diophanes. The latter, however, used to use a long rectangular stamp in a single or double frame[359]. Neither is represented in the Pergamon deposit nor in any other well-dated group from the end of the 3rd and beginning of the 2nd cent. B.C., thus both should presumably be considered of a later date.

The stamps of both producers are rather infrequent[360].

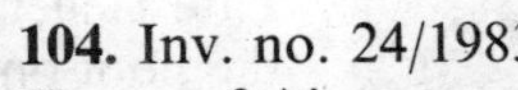

104. Inv. no. 24/1983
House of Aion, room 3, above mosaic floor level
Diam.: 3 cm
Circular stamp with a representation of a rose and encircling inscription:

Δαμοκράτευς rose

Damokrates I was one of the most active producers of period III. Grace considers him to be the one who introduced the habit of using small subsidiary stamps — a small flower of the rose — around 188 B.C. She also suggests that he was the father of another known Rhodian producer — Aristokles, and perhaps of Hippokrates as well[361]. The stamps recorded at Pergamon[362] and Villanova[363] accompany stamps of many eponyms of the period 188—183 B.C.: Agemachos[364], Aristokrates II[365], Ariston II[366], Kallikratidas II[367], Kleonymos II[368],

[355] Grace-Savvatianou, pp. 316—317, no. E 45.
[356] Loc. cit.
[357] Nilsson, no. 149; Šelov 1975, no. 305; Crowfoot, p. 383; Breccia, p. 30, no. 68.
[358] Nilsson, p. 161, no. 160; Grace 1952, p. 526; Breccia, p. 30, nos. 70—71; Crowfoot, p. 383.
[359] Nilsson, p. 161 and no. 180; Breccia, p. 31; Šelov 1975, no. 327.
[360] See notes 353 and 354 above.
[361] Grace-Savvatianou, pp. 280, 295 note 1, 380, nos. E 15, E 24, E 42, E 66. See also Grace 1985, p. 8f.; Grace 1968, p. 175.
[362] Schuchhardt, nos. 997—1000.
[363] Maiuri, pp. 258 and 262.
[364] Paris 1914, p. 322.
[365] Badal'janc, p. 164.
[366] Loc. cit.
[367] Gentili, p. 29 and p. 14, no. 5.
[368] Badal'janc, p. 164.

Nikasagoras I[369], Pratophanes[370] and Philodamos[371]. Thanks to this Grace could date Damokrates I to this period, that is the years 188—183 B.C.[372]

Stamps of Damokrates belong to the most common of Rhodian stamps[373].

105. Inv. no. 19/1977
Villa of Theseus, layer V of well in room 69
Diam.: 3 cm
Δαμοκράτευς rose

Stamp of Damokrates. See no. 104 above.

106. Inv. no. 18/1989
Late Hellenistic House, south of the wall limiting the pool on the east, in stone debris fill
Diam.: 3 cm
Δαμοκράτευς rose

Stamp of Damokrates. See no. 104 above.

107. Inv. no. 31/1986
Villa of Theseus, western wing, sector 9/2/85, upper layer
Dimensions: 4.5 × 1.8 cm
Rectangular stamp with one line of inscription:
Διοδότου

The name of the producer Diodotos is recorded in Pergamon[374] placing him in period III, that is 210—175 B.C.

The name of Diodotos is not frequent among Rhodian stamps[375].

[369] Grace 1985, p. 45, no. 2; Grace-Savvatianou, p. 306, no. E 15.
[370] Maiuri, p. 258, XXVI.
[371] Grace 1950, p. 135 note 2, and p. 145, nos. 72—73.
[372] Grace 1985, pp. 8—10, 12—13.
[373] Nilsson, no. 165; Paris 1914, p. 308, XXX-XXXI; Porro 1916, p. 154, no. 84; Grace 1952, p. 526; Calvet 1972, nos. 40—42; Calvet 1982, nos. 38—41; Sztetyłło 1976, nos. 77—82; Grace 1934, pp. 238—239, nos. 90—92; Grace 1950, p. 145, no. 73; Pridik, p. 24, nos. 558—573; Šelov 1975, p. 211, nos. 307—314; Šelov 1956, p. 137; Levi 1964, p. 269, nos. 226—234; Mirčev, nos. 132—134; Lazarov 1977, p. 35, no. 30; Gramatopol-Poenaru Bordea, Tomis, no. 66; Breccia, p. 31; Empereur 1977, nos. 29—34; Reisner, p. 311; Macalister, p. 356; Crowfoot, p. 383; Sztetyłło 1975, nos. 64—65; Sztetyłło 1978, no. 25; Sztetyłło 1983, no. 44; Sztetyłło 1990, nos. 21—22; Börker, no. 24; Gentili, no. 79; Pellegrini, p. 222, no. 502; Brugnone, pp. 53—55, nos. 78—83; Sztetyłło 1963, p. 337.
[374] Schuchhardt, no. 1001.
[375] Nilsson, no. 173; Grace 1952, p. 526; Grace 1950, no. 1; Šelov 1975, nos. 319—320; Lazarov 1977, p. 36, no. 34; Sztetyłło 1976, p. 43, nos. 83—85; Breccia, p. 31; Sztetyłło 1978, p. 275, no. 26; Crowfoot, p. 383; Le Roy, BIFAO 84, p. 311, no. 12; Sztetyłło 1990, nos. 23—24.

108. Inv. no. 21/1983
Villa of Theseus, northern wing, sector 5/82/83 (Hellenistic context)
Dimensions: 3.5 × 1 cm
Rectangular stamp with a one-line inscription:
Δίου

Stamps with the name of Dios have been found in the dated deposits at Pergamon[376] and Olbia[377] making it possible to place this producer in the end of the 3rd and beginning of 2nd cent. B.C. The dating is confirmed by the concurrence of Dios' stamps with the stamps of eponyms of 210—175 B.C., including Ariston II[378], Thestor[379], Kallikrates II[380] and Kleonymos[381].

Stamps of the producer Dios are often found on various sites of Rhodes, Delos, Cyprus, the coast of the Black Sea and other regions of the ancient world[382].

109. Inv. no. 39/1980
Villa of Theseus, northwestern section of the residence
Dimensions: 3.4 × 1.2 cm
Δίου

Stamp of Dios. See no. 108 above.

110. Inv. no. 38/1986
House of Aion, room 3, a layer of ashes ca 1.20—1.60 m down from the surface
Dimensions: 4 × 1.8 cm
Rectangular stamp with one line of inscription:
Δωροθέου

Since the name of the producer Dorotheos was found in the Pergamon deposit, it was possible to date him accordingly to period III, that is 210—175 B.C.[383]

Stamps with the name of Dorotheos are not frequently discovered in the archaeological record[384].

[376] Schuchhardt, no. 1006.
[377] Levi 1964, p. 269, nos. 236—246.
[378] Šelov 1975, p. 96, no. 326; Badal'janc, p. 164. Grace dates Ariston II to around 178 B.C., see Grace 1985, p. 8.
[379] Grace 1963, p. 323 and 334, no. 9, fig. 1, 9; Grace, Amphoras, fig. 62; Grace-Savvatianou, p. 294; Badal'janc, p. 164.
[380] Levi 1964, p. 272, nos. 334—335, pl. XXII; Nachtergael, p. 52; Šelov 1975, p. 56; Badal'janc, p. 164.
[381] Crowfoot, p. 387.
[382] Nilsson, p. 179; Paris 1914, p. 309, XXXV; Porro 1916, p. 114, no. 86; Grace 1952, p. 526; Grace 1934, p. 227, no. 45; Calvet 1978, p. 225, no. 18; Sztetyłło 1976, no. 86; Pridik, p. 25, nos. 590—596; Levi 1964, p. 269, nos. 236—246; Šelov 1975, p. 96, no. 326; Lazarov 1977, p. 36, no. 36; Gramatopol-Poenaru Bordea, Dacia XIII, p. 234, no. 756; Breccia, p. 31; Reisner, p. 311; Macalister, p. 356; Crowfoot, p. 383; Gentili, p. 59, no. 84; Pellegrini, p. 224, no. 211; Brugnone, p. 56, no. 85.

111. Inv. no. 30/1985
Villa of Theseus, in a pit in the northwestern section of the residence
Dimension: 3.5 × 1.5 cm
Rectangular stamp with one line of inscription:
Δωροθέου

Stamp of the producer Dorotheos. See no. 110 above.

112. Inv. no. 6/1979
Villa of Theseus, room 86, upper layer
Dimensions: 3.5 × 1.2 cm
'Εδυμίου? [reversed?]

Stamp of Edymios(?). No analogies were discovered; quite probably from the second half of the 2nd cent. B.C. The stamp may belong to the producer Aineas placed in period III, see no. 84

113. Inv. no. 31/1980
Villa of Theseus, northern wing, upper layer
Dimensions: 4.5 × 1.5 cm
'Καρνείου
'Επίγονος

Stamp of Epigonos, month Karneios.

Epigonos is placed in period II (ca 240—210 B.C.) preceding the so-called "Pergamene" period[385]. Not only is the lack of his stamps in Pergamon in favour of this, but also the similarity of his stamps — in form including the shape of a leaf — to the stamps of eponyms of that period[386]. He cooperated with some of them, e.g. Xenostratos[387] and Similinos[388], as combinations of stamps prove. In contrast to the stamps of other producers of the second half of the 3rd cent. B.C., the stamps of Epigonos are frequently encountered[389].

[383] Schuchhardt, no. 1013.

[384] Nilsson, no. 186; Pridik, p. 26, nos. 606—608; Šelov 1975, nos. 331—333; Grace 1952, p. 526; Calvet 1972, no. 43; Calvet 1982, p. 23, no. 45; Gramatopol-Poenaru Bordea, Dacia XIII, no. 757; Börker, nos. 20—21; Crowfoot, p. 383.

[385] Grace 1956, no. 84.

[386] Nilsson, pp. 105—106 and 151.

[387] Nilsson, loc. cit.; Pridik 1926, pp. 318, 320, 324,

[388] Loc. cit. and Nilsson, no. 376, 1; Grace 1934, no. 75; Badal'janc, p. 166.

[389] Nilsson, no. 192; Paris 1914, p. 309, XXXIX; Grace 1934, no. 75; Grace 1956, no. 84; Lenger 1955, no. 1; Grace 1952, p. 526; Sztetyłło 1976, no. 7; Šelov 1975, no. 342; Bingen, no. 3; Sztetyłło 1983, no. 3; Sztetyłło 1975, no. 16; Börker, no. 19; Crowfoot, p. 383.

114. Inv. no. 10/1976
Villa of Theseus, sector V/76, upper layer
Dimensions: 4.1 × 1.6 cm
'Επικράτευς
'Αγριανίου

Stamp of the producer Epikrates, month Agrianios.

His period is determined primarily on the grounds of a combination with the eponym Pausanias III[390]. His are not frequently found stamps[391].

115. Inv. no. 38/1986
House of Aion, room 3, layer of ashes
Dimensions: 4.8 × 2.4 cm
Rectangular stamp with two lines of inscription and a representation of a caduceus lying horizontally to the right below the legend.
Εὐκλεί-   caduceus
του

The stamps of producer Eukleitos feature a great variety of form and are very frequent. One of the most characteristic elements is the caduceus shown lying horizontally. Eukleitos belongs to a group of producers whose activity falls before the year 150 B.C., that is in the end of period IV and at the beginning of period V[392]; this is because his stamps have not been discovered in well-dated deposits of the end of the 3rd and beginning of the 2nd cent. B.C. and because they have been noted in combination with the stamps of eponyms of the younger period. The eponyms in question include Aleximachos[393], Astymedes II[394], Thersandros[395], Nikasagoras II[396] and Timodikos[397].

Stamps of Eukleitos have been noted in various regions and they are among the most common of Rhodian stamps[398].

[390] Grace 1934, nos. 4—5. See also Grace-Savvatianou, pp. 304—305, no. E 12; Grace 1952, p. 537, no. 23; Badal'janc, p. 166.
[391] Nilsson, no. 194; Paris 1914, p. 309, XL.
[392] Grace 1985, p. 13 note 23, ca. 141—135 B.C.
[393] Badal'janc, p. 165; Šelov 1975, nos. 87, 351; Lazarov 1977, p. 36, no. 39.
[394] Šelov 1975, p. 101, no. 351; Grace 1965, p. 7 note 6; Nicolaou-Empereur, pp. 526—527, no. 11.
[395] Grace 1962, p. 115, no. 7; Nicolaou-Empereur, p. 529, no. 14.
[396] Macalister, p. 537, no. 216; Grace 1962, p. 116.
[397] Porro, p. 383, nos. 17—18, p. 385, nos. 41—42; Grace 1934, p. 219, mentions also the combination Eukleitos — Aristakos.
[398] Nilsson, no. 203; Paris, p. 160, XLIV; Paris 1914, p. 309, XLII; Grace 1952, p. 526; Sztetyłło 1976, nos. 90—91; Sztetyłło 1984, no. 11; Šelov 1975, nos. 344—353; Lazarov 1977, p. 37, no. 46; Breccia, p. 33, no. 89; Empereur 1977, p. 215, no. 45; Sztetyłło 1975, nos. 72—73; Sztetyłło 1990, nos. 41—47; Macalister, p. 357; Crowfoot, p. 383; Sztetyłło 1983, p. 96, no. 77.

116. Inv. no. 29/1986
Villa of Theseus, southern wing, sector 1/86, upper layer (the western end of the wing)
Dimensions: 4 × 1.7 cm
The end of a one-line inscription has been preserved together with a representation of a caduceus shown lying horizontally below the text.
[Εὐκλεί]του caduceus

This may be a stamp of Eukleitos considering the name ending and the representation which is characteristic of this producer. See no. 115 above.

117. Inv. no. 36/1978
Villa of Theseus, northeastern part of the residence
Dimensions: 4.1 × 1.5 cm
[Εὐκλεί]του caduceus to the right

Stamp of Eukleitos. See no. 115 above.

118. Inv. no. 38/1978
Villa of Theseus, northeastern part of the residence, upper layer
Dimensions: 4.2 × 1.6 cm
[Εὐκλ]είτου caduceus to the right

Stamp of Eukleitos, see above.

119. Inv. no. 2/1985
Villa of Theseus, western wing, room 22, upper layer
Dimensions: 4.1 × 1.7 cm
[Εὐκλεί]του caduceus

Stamp of Eukleitos, see above.

120. Inv. no. 32/1987
Late Hellenistic House, sector 13/87, upper layer
Dimensions: 5 × 3 cm
Rectangular stamp with one line of inscription:
῾Ηρακλείτου

Stamps with the name of the producer Herakleitos were dated to the end of the 3rd and beginning of the 2nd cent. B.C. on the grounds of finds from Pergamon[399] and Olbia[400]. A closer analysis of this group of stamps permitted Grace to place Herakleitos in the period 188—183 B.C. owing to a concurrence with the stamps of the eponym Nikasagoras I[4012] known to have been active in this period[402].

Stamps of Herakleitos have been recorded in Rhodes, Delos, Egypt, areas of the Black Sea and the ancient Near East[403].

121. Inv. no. IP/1981
Surface find from the vicinity of the Villa of Theseus
Dimensions: 3.6 × 1.5 cm
῾Ηρακ- bunch of grapes on the right
λέων

There are no analogies for this stamp of Herakleon. The use of a token especially popular from the middle of the 2nd cent. B.C. suggests a dating in this period for our stamp.

See Sztetyłło 1976, no. 187.

122. Inv. no. 1/1980
Villa of Theseus, sector I/80, upper layer
Dimensions: 3.7 × 1.4 cm
[Θεμί-] bunch of grapes on the right
σωνος

There are no grounds except the token for dating this stamp and consequently the producer Themison; like the previous stamp, it may possibly originate from the middle of the 2nd cent. B.C.

See Šelov 1975, no. 362; Nilsson, no. 230; Paris, p. 310, XLVI; Crowfoot, p. 383; Sztetyłło 1984, no. 15.

399 Schuchhardt, nos. 1019—1021.
400 Levi 1964, nos. 250—258.
401 Badal'janc, p. 163.
402 Grace 1985, p. 8f. It is Grace's opinion that the small subsidiary stamp used by this eponym constitutes an argument in favour of such a dating, considering that such stamps were introduced around 188 B.C.
403 Nilsson, no. 225; Paris 1914, p. 310, XLV; Grace 1952, p. 527; Šelov 1975, no. 74; Empereur 1977, no. 49; Sztetyłło 1975, no. 74; Sztetyłło 1978, no. 29; Sztetyłło 1990, no. 26; Börker, no. 22; Crowfoot, p. 383.

123. Inv. no. 15/1988
Late Hellenistic House, in the lower part of the debris fill
Diam.: 3 cm
'Ιάσωνος 'Αρταμιτίου rose

Stamp of the producer Iason, month Artamitios.

Iason's stamps discovered at Pergamon[404] place him in the group of producers from period III, but rather in the end of that period as the concurring stamps of eponyms prove. The eponyms in question are Andrias[405], Aristodamos II[406] and Kallikratidas II[407], all of whom are dated to the beginning of the 2nd cent. B.C.

Iason's stamps are not very widespread[408].

124. Inv. no. 21/1988
Late Hellenistic House, sector 16/S, below the top of the latitudinal wall
Dimensions: 3.7 × 1.8 cm
'Ιάσωνος flower on the right

Stamp of the producer Iason with an atrribute in the lower left corner considered by Nilsson to be characteristic of this producer. See above.

125. Inv. no. IP 1982
Surface find from the Villa of Theseus
Dimensions: 2.8 × 1.5 cm
Rectangular stamp with one line of inscription, preserved fragmentarily.
['Ιέρ] ωνος

Hieron appears to be a contemporary of Eukleitos for the stamps of both appear on amphorae stamped also by one eponym, Timodikos[409]. Furthermore, the stamps of both have the same shape of a long rectangle and both used the same representation: a caduceus lying horizontally. Even so, the dating is not beyond doubt. Hieron's stamps have been found in the Pergamon deposit[410], suggesting a possible date at the beginning of the 2nd cent. B.C., corroborated by the similarity to the stamps of Eukleitos who was active before 150 B.C. At the

[404] Schuchhardt, nos. 1037, 1039.
[405] Nilsson, no. 49, 4.
[406] Bleckmann 1907, p. 22 and 31; Bleckmann 1912, p. 251; Badal'janc, p. 165.
[407] Pridik 1926, pp. 315, 320, 325; Badal'janc, p. 165.
[408] Nilsson, no. 247; Pridik, no. 659; Šelov 1975, nos. 365—366; Grace 1952, p. 527; Grace 1950, no. 37; Sztetyłło 1976, no. 158; Sztetyłło 1975, nos. 75—76; Breccia, p. 35; Empereur 1977, nos. 59—60; Crowfoot, p. 383; Le Roy, BIFAO 84, nos. 13—14.
[409] Porro, p. 383, nos. 17—18, p. 385, nos. 41—42. Grace 1965, p. 7 note 8, mentions the combination Hieron — Astymedes.
[410] Schuchhardt, nos. 1050—1051.

same time there exist combinations of Hieron with the eponym Dionysios[411], the latter also being represented in the Pergamon collection[412]. Other combinations which should be mentioned are with the eponyms Anaxandros and Astymedes II[413] and they also place Hieron's activity in the period before 150 B.C. This does not contradict the fact the name of Hieron concurs with that of the eponym Timodikos who is also known from amphorae stamped by Eukleitos and who was active in the second half of the 2nd cent. B.C. Either the activity period of producer or eponym was extended into the second half of the 2nd cent. B.C. or we have here an example of homonyms in one case or in both[414].

Hieron's stamps are especially popular on Rhodes, Delos, the Black Sea areas and regions of the ancient Near East[415].

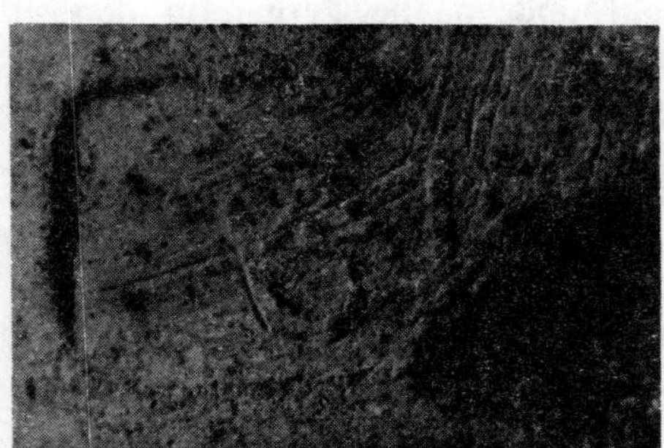

126. Inv. no. 2/1980
From the northeastern part of the Villa of Theseus
Dimensions: 3.5 × 1.6 cm

'Ιμᾶ caduceus horizontally

Stamp of Imas assuming the reconstruction of the badly obliterated stamp is correct.

Imas was one of the more active Rhodian producers of periods III—IV, corroborated by the concurrence of his stamps with those of the eponyms: Autokrates[416], Damainetos[417], Thersandros[418], Pythodoros[419], Pausanias III[420] and Timourrodos[421]. His activity is comprised between the years 175—136 B.C.[422]

Stamps of Imas are often recorded among the finds[423].

[411] Such a combination is mentioned by Šelov 1975, p. 104, no. 366, note 563. See also Badal'janc, p. 164.
[412] Schuchhardt, nos. 1003—1004.
[413] Nicolaou-Empereur, pp. 525—526, nos. 9—10.
[414] Grace 1965, p. 7 note 8; Nachtergael, pp. 50—51; Brugnone, p. 41, no. 56 and notes 315—316.
[415] Nilsson, no. 252; Porro 1916, p. 117, no. 110; Grace 1952, p. 527; Šelov 1975, nos. 366—367; Lazarov 1977, p. 38, no. 65; Breccia, p. 36, no. 109; Sztetyłło 1983, nos. 48—49; Le Roy, p. 241, no. 9; Sztetyłło 1975, nos. 77—78; Crowfoot, p. 383.
[416] Grace, Amphoras, fig. 31; Badal'janc, p. 165.
[417] Nilsson, p. 115; Bleckmann 1907, pp. 22 and 32.
[418] Porro, nos. 37—38.
[419] Porro, nos. 15—16.
[420] Bleckmann 1907, p. 22 and 31.
[421] Loc. cit.
[422] Grace-Savvatianou, nos. E 7—E 9.
[423] Nilsson, no. 254; Paris 1914, p. 310, LI; Grace 1952, p. 527; Calvet 1972, no. 56; Sztetyłło 1976, no. 191; Pridik, nos. 669—672; Šelov 1975, no. 368; Gramatopol-Poenaru Bordea, Dacia XIII, nos. 1147—1148; Empereur 1977, no. 63; Sztetyłło 1975, no. 137; Sztetyłło 1978, nos. 45—46; Sztetyłło 1990, nos. 53—54; Crowfoot, p. 383; Reisner, p. 312; Macalister, p. 358; Brugnone, no. 90.

127. Inv. no. IP/1981
Villa of Theseus, X/81, upper layer
Dimensions: 3.5 × 1.4 cm
'Ιμᾶ caduceus horizontally

Stamp of Imas. See above.

128. Inv. no. 12/1982 P
Surface find from the Villa of Theseus
Diam.: 3 cm
Circular stamp with a representation of a rose and encircling inscription:
'Ιπποκράτευς rose

The producer Hippokrates worked in period III as his stamps found in the Pergamon deposit confirm[424]. In my opinion, he belongs to the group of producers who should be dated to the end of this period and the beginning of period IV, that is before the year 150 B.C., for his stamps concur with the stamps of such eponyms of the turn of periods III and IV as Aristodamos[425], Eudamos[426], Hieron I[427], Xenophantos[428], Pausanias III[429] and Pythogenes and Theaidetos[430].

Hippokrates was most probably the son of the known — considering the number of his stamps that are recorded — Rhodian producer Damokrates I and brother of the equally famous producer Aristokles. He was also, according to Grace, one of those Rhodian producers who took after Damokrates I the habit of supplementing their main stamp with an additional small stamp[431].

Stamps of Hippokrates were found on Rhodes, Delos, Cyprus, Crete, in Athens, areas of the Black Sea coast and of the ancient Near East[432].

[424] Schuchhardt, no. 1052.

[425] Bleckmann 1907, p. 22 and 32; Nilsson, p. 115 note 1; Calvet 1982, no. 8; Badal'janc, p. 164. See the dating of Aristodamos to the years 182—176 B.C., Grace 1985, p. 8 and p. 45 no. 3.

[426] Badal'janc, p. 164. On the basis of data from Tarsus and Delos Grace places Eudamos in period IV, see Grace 1950, p. 142; no. 43, and Grace 1952, p. 529.

[427] Badal'janc, p. 164. Grace dates Hieron I to the beginning of the 2nd cent. B.C., more precisely in 198 B.C. See Grace 1950, p. 136, no. 71, and Grace 1985, p. 23 note 60.

[428] Bleckmann 1907, p. 22 and 32; Grace 1934, p. 219; Badal'janc, p. 164. According to Grace, Xenophantos II worked at the beginning of the 2nd cent. B.C. and cooperated with the producer Diskos among others. See Grace 1950, p. 136, p. 140, no. 21a—b. See also Grace-Savvatianou, p. 294 note 2.

[429] Badal'janc, p. 164. Grace attributes Pausanias II to period IV, see Grace 1953, p. 118 and note 5. See also Grace-Savvatianou, p. 298 and 304, no. E 12; Nachtergael, p. 54, no. 22.

[430] Hall, p. 390, 5041, and Grace 1934, p. 219; Badal'janc, p. 164; for the combination Hippokrates — Pythogenes, see Nicolaou-Empereur, p. 520, no. 6.

129. Inv. no. 27/1986
House of Aion, room 3, in wall debris (ca 0.80 m down from the surface)
Dimensions: 4 × 1 cm
Rectangular stamp with oblitered surface, but with the first letter of one line of inscription preserved and a faint image to the right of the text, possibly a bunch of grapes.

Λ[ίνου] bunch of grapes(?)

If the reconstruction is correct, this is a stamp of the producer Linos. He is known to appear together with the stamps of the eponym Nikasagoras I who also used small subsidiary stamps[433]. On this basis Linos may be dated to around 185 B.C.[434]

Linos' stamps are not among the more frequent Rhodian stamps found on archaeological sites[435].

130. Inv. no. IP/1979
Surface find from the vicinity of the Villa of Theseus
Dimensions: 4.1 × 1.2 cm

Λίνου bunch of grapes

Stamp of Linos, see above.

131. Inv. no. 36/1983
Villa of Theseus, sounding I in sector 11/82/83 in the northwestern part of the residence. The stamp was preserved on one handle of a Rhodian amphora, the other handle of which bore the stamp of an eponym, unfortunately completely obliterated. Only the rectangular shape of the latter has remained.
Dimensions: 3.4 × 1.5 cm
Rectangular stamp with two lines of inscription:

Μαρσύα
'Αγριανίου

Stamp of the producer Marsyas, month Agrianios.

431 Grace, Kyme 1, p. 94, A 3; Grace 1985, p. 10; Grace 1934, p. 239, no. 93 a—b. See also Šelov 1975, no. 369 and note 569; Šelov 1966, p. 666.

432 Nilsson, no. 255; Porro 1916, p. 117, no. 113; Grace 1952, p. 527; Levi, Festos, p. 576, no. 5; Calvet 1982, p. 57, no. 58 (with subsidiary stamps); Sztetyłło 1976, nos. 94—95; Grace 1934, p. 239 and 240, nos. 93—94; Pridik, p. 28, nos. 673—680; Šelov 1956, pp. 137—140, nos. 3, 4, 19, 29, 30, 63—66; Šelov 1975, nos. 369—375; Breccia, p. 36, no. 113; Reisner, p. 312; Macalister, p. 358; Crowfoot, p. 383; Sztetyłło 1975, p. 181, no. 79; Criscuolo, nos. 109—111; Gentili, p. 68, no. 122; Pellegrini, p. 233, nos. 286—290; Brugnone, pp. 60—61, nos. 91—94.

433 Maiuri, p. 268, no. 1; Badal'janc, p. 165, mentions the eponym Anaxandros beside Nikasagoras I.

434 A general chronological frame for the activity of Nikasagoras I is provided by the discovery of his stamps in the Pergamon deposit. See Schuchhardt, nos. 1139—1154. Grace narrows this down to around 188 B.C., see Grace 1985, p. 8.

435 Nilsson, no. 286; Maiuri, p. 258; Grace 1952, p. 527; Šelov 1975, nos. 392—397; Lazarov 1977, p. 38, no. 76; Breccia, p. 39; Crowfoot, p. 383.

Marsyas is a producer whose name often appears on Rhodian amphorae. His stamps are specially frequent, in Šelov's opinion, on sites from the northern coasts of the Black Sea where over 150 examples have been recorded[436].

His stamps have also been found in the Pergamon deposit[437] suggesting the period of the end of the 3rd and beginning of the 2nd cent. B.C. for his activity. A more exact dating to the years around 197 or 195 B.C. was possible thanks to the concurrence of his stamps with those of eponyms of period IV, a fact that narrowed down the years of Marsyas' activity to the first two decades of the 2nd cent. B.C. Since among the eponyms there were officials who acted in the last years of period III or the very beginning of period IV, Marsyas could be dated to around 197 or 195 B.C. Of the known combinations one should mention the eponyms Ariston II[438], Damokles II and Kleonymos II[439] (all three from the turn of periods III and IV), and Peisistratos[440] and Heragoras[441], both from the beginning of period IV.

Stamps of Marsyas, who included the name of the month beside his own, are very widespread and numerous on archaeological sites[442].

132. Inv. no. 10/1988
Late Hellenistic House, in stone debris fill (ca 0.90—1 m down from the surface)
Dimensions: 2 × 1.2 cm
Μαρ[σύα]
'Αγρια[νίου]

Stamp of Marsyas, month Agrianios. See above.

[436] Šelov 1975, pp. 109—110.
[437] Schuchhardt, nos. 1122—1134.
[438] Dunand II, p. 801, no. 15786.
[439] Bleckmann 1907, p. 32; Bleckmann 1912, p. 251; Grace 1934, p. 219; Badal'janc, p. 165; Nicolaou-Empereur, p. 515, no. 2. See also Nachtergael, pp. 34—35; Grace 1985, p. 44.
[440] Grace 1934, p. 219; Nilsson, p. 530, no. 2; Bleckmann 1912, p. 250; Grace-Savvatianou, p. 314, no. E 37; Badal'janc, p. 165; see also Nachtergael, p. 35.
[441] Sztetyłło 1976, p. 44, no. 92, p. 48, no. 109. See also the combination Marsyas — eponym Aristomachos, in; Grace-Savvatianou, no. E 37, dating to before 150 B.C.
[442] Nilsson, no. 298; Paris 1914, p. 314, LIX; Porro 1916, p. 118; Levi 1964, p. 270, nos. 278—291; Pridik, pp. 29, 30, nos. 715—730; Šelov 1975, nos. 401—404; Mirčev, no. 142; Lazarov 1977, p. 38, no. 71; Gramatopol-Poenaru Bordea, Dacia XIII, p. 235, nos. 766—767, p. 267, no. 1177; Grace 1952, p. 527; Calvet 1972, no. 53; Calvet 1982, p. 28, n. 68; I. Nicolaou, *RDAC* 1970, p. 160, no. 21; Sztetyłło 1976, nos. 109—112; Breccia, p. 39, no. 132; Empereur 1977, p. 222, nos. 67—68; Sztetyłło 1975, nos. 88—89; Sztetyłło 1978, p. 279, no. 31; Nachtergael, nos. 9—10; Crowfoot, p. 383; Criscuolo, nos. 112—113; Gentili, p. 73, no. 134; Pellegrini, p. 239, no. 31; Brugnone, pp. 62—63, no. 96.

133. Inv. no. 18/1983
Villa of Theseus, northern wing, sector 5/82/83 (Hellenistic layers below the latitudinal wall)
Dimensions: 3.5 × 1.5 cm
Rectangular stamp with two lines of inscription, the text in reverse.
Μαρσύα
Δαλίου

Stamp of Marsyas, month Dalios. See above.

134. Inv. no. 11/1975
Villa of Theseus, western wing
Dimensions: 3.4 × 1.5 cm
Δαλίου
Μαρσύα

Stamp of Marsyas, month Dalios. See above.

135. Inv. no. 12/1975
Villa of Theseus, western wing
Dimensions: 3.4 × 1.5 cm
Μαρσύα
Καρνείου

Stamp of Marsyas, month Karneios. See above.

136. Inv. no. 77/1986
House of Aion, room 3, in debris from room 4
Dimensions: 4 × 2.7 cm
Rectangular stamp with one line of inscription:
Μεν[εκρά]τευς

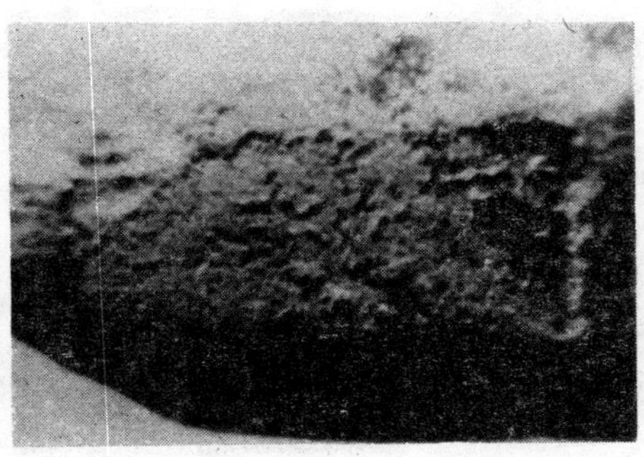

This stamp with the name of a producer Menekrates should presumably be connected with a Rhodian producer active in the years 182—176 B.C., a date confirmed by the concurrence of stamps of the eponym Aristeidas II from this period[443]. There was also another Rhodian producer of this name who stamped amphorae together with the eponym Mytion[444]. However, judging by the date of the

[443] Šelov 1975, no. 405 and no. 40; Badal'janc, p. 165. Grace dates the eponym Aristeidas II to the years 182—176 B.C., cf. Grace-Savvatianou, p. 291 and 314, no. E 11. Grace also believes that Aristeidas held the office of priest of Helios in the year 180 B.C., see Grace 1985, p. 8. See also Schuchhardt, nos. 878—884.
[444] Grace 1934, p. 225, no. 38; Grace 1956, p. 143, no. 98; Grace 1950, p. 140, no. 15; Badal'janc, p. 165.

eponym Mytion, Menekrates I should rather be placed in period II[445].

Stamps of Menekrates, both I and II not always strictly distinguished, are not often encountered on sites yielding Rhodian stamps[446].

137. Inv. no. IP/1981
Found near the Villa of Theseus
Dimensions: 3.9 × 2.6 cm

Μην[εκράτευς]

Stamp of Menekrates(?), see above.

138. Inv. no. 12/1988
Late Hellenistic House, bottom part of rubble fill
Diam.: 3.5 cm

Μηνοδ[ώρου]   head of Helios

Presumably a stamp with the name of the producer Menodoros. Grace dates him to period VI, i.e. end of the 2nd and beginning of the 1st cent. B.C.[447] Šelov does not exclude the existence of another producer of this name active at a later time, that is presumably the first half of the 2nd cent. B.C.[448]

Stamps of Menodoros are rare[449].

139. Inv. no. 2/1989
Villa of Theseus, sounding in the eastern corridor, layer 3
Dimensions: 3.5 × 2 cm

Surface of stamp obliterated, name in two lines preserved only fragmentarily, presumably that of the producer Mentor or Menippos.

Μέν-
[τορ]ου(?)

Stamps of Mentor or Menippos are extremely rare. A few have been found on the Athenian Agora[450], examples have been recorded in Alexandria[451], on Delos and in Samaria[452]; Nilsson registers

[445] See note 444.
[446] Nilsson, no. 305; Grace 1934, p. 225, no. 38; Grace 1950, p.. 140, no. 15; Sztetyłło 1976, nos. 159—160; Säflund, p. 14, no. 8; Pridik, p. 30, nos. 731—732; Šelov 1975, no. 405; Lazarov 1977, p. 38, no. 78; Gramatopol-Poenaru Bordea, Dacia XIII, p. 235, no. 768; Empereur 1977, no. 69; Börker, p. 34, no. 2; Crowfoot, p. 383.
[447] Grace-Savvatianou, p. 310, E 28.
[448] Šelov 1975, no. 406.
[449] Nilsson, no. 312; Breccia, p. 39.
[450] Grace 1934, p. 223, no. 28; Grace 1952, p. 527.
[451] Breccia, p. 38.
[452] Crowfoot, p. 383.

one stamp preserving also the name of the month Hyakinthios. The stamp registered by Botti, if the reconstruction is correct, shows stars beside the name of Menippos[453]. Mentor's stamps do not appear in well-dated assemblages of the end of the 3rd and first half of the 2nd cent. B.C. and there are no names of eponyms to confirm a dating for him. It would seem that he was active in the second half of the 2nd cent. B.C.

140. Inv. no. 34/1978
Villa of Theseus, northern wing
Dimensions: 4.5 × 1.5 cm
Μίδα bunch of grapes

Midas, whose activity falls in the years 146—108 B.C.[454], was one of the more prolific producers. He cooperated with the eponyms Aristogenes[455], Aristokles[456], Alexiadas[457], Teisamenos[458] and Klenostratos[459].

Stamps of Midas are often encountered in the material[460].

141. Inv. no. IP/1981
Found near the Villa of Theseus
Dimensions: 4.2 × 1.2 cm
Μίδα bunch of grapes and caduceus

Stamp of Midas. See above.

142. Inv. no. IP/1979
Villa of Theseus, room 79
Dimensions: 3 × 1.7 cm
Μόσ[χου]

There are some difficulties in dating the producer Moschos in view of the absence of his stamps from well-dated groups of finds. Olbia is an exception on the grounds of which Šelov suggests a dating to the pre-Pergamon period[461], but there is no other

[453] Botti, "Notice des monuments exposés au Musée Gréco-Romain d'Alexandrie", *Alexandrie 1883, Service des Antiquités de l'Egypte*, p. 240, no. 4323; Breccia, p. 36; Crowfoot, p. 383.
[454] For Midas and his acivity, see Grace 1985, pp. 9, 10 and 42; Grace supplied the information that Midas cooperated with 12 eponyms.
[455] Bleckmann 1907, p. 32 and 33.
[456] Badal'janc, p. 165; Grace 1953, p. 121 note 4.
[457] See note 456 above.
[458] Nicolaou-Empereur, p. 527, no. 12.
[459] Grace-Savvatianou, no. E 45.
[460] Nilsson, no. 314; Grace 1952, p. 527; Paris, p. 163, LXV; Šelov 1975, nos. 407—411; Sztetyłło 1976, nos. 194—198; Sztetyłło 1984, no. 14; Breccia, p. 40; Empereur 1977, nos. 70—71; Sztetyłło 1975, nos. 140—143; Sztetyłło 1990, nos. 74—75; Sztetyłło 1983, no. 85; Crowfoot, p. 383; Gramatopol-Poenaru Bordea, Dacia XIII, no. 768.
[461] Šelov 1975, nos. 413—416.

data to corroborate this[462]. Rather, he should be placed in the post-Pergamon period, a view that is backed up by the characteristic features of the stamps.

Stamps of Moschos are not among the frequent finds[463].

143. Inv. no. 8/1976
Villa of Theseus, sector III/76
Dimensions: 4.3 × 1.7 cm
Μουσαίου bunch of grapes

Stamp of Mousaios. The absence of combinations with stamp of eponyms excludes any dating attempts. Grace places him in period VI on the basis of the context of finds from the Agora[464].

These stamps are not over frequently discovered[465].

144. Inv. no. IP/1981
Surface find from the vicinity of the Villa of Theseus
Dimensions: 4.3 × 1.8 cm
Μουσαίου bunch of grapes

Stamp of Mousaios. See above.

145. Inv. no. 16/1983
Villa of Theseus, southern wing, sector 10/82/83, room 53, upper layer
Dimensions: 3.5 × 1 cm
Rectangular stamp with one line of inscription. Lunate *sigma*.

Νάνις

Although stamps of Nanis were found in Pergamon, permitting a date in the end of the 3rd or the beginning of the 2nd cent. B.C., Grace is of the opinion that this eponym worked in the last years of the "Pergamon" period and continued into the second quarter of the 2nd cent. B.C.[466]

Bleckmann cites a combination of Nanis and the eponym Aristeidas, but there is some uncertainty

[462] Nachtergael, pp. 24—25, no. 4.
[463] Nilsson, no. 318; Pridik 1926, p. 329; Levi 1964, no. 293; Nachtergael, no. 4 (a discussion of the distribution of the stamps). See Breccia, p. 40; Gramatopol-Poenaru Bordea, Dacia XIII, no. 770; Mirčev, no. 145.
[464] Grace-Savvatianou, p. 311, no. E 29.
[465] Nilsson, no. 319; Grace 1952, p. 527; Calvet 1978, no. 33; Sztetyłło 1976, no. 231; Šelov 1975, nos. 417—421; Gramatopol-Poenaru Bordea, Dacia XIII, no. 771; Mirčev, no. 146; Sztetyłło 1975, no. 145.
[466] Schuchhardt, no. 1137; Grace-Savvatianou, p. 304, no. E 1.

about the validity of the reading of the eponym's name[467].

Stamps of Nanis were recorded on many sites, i.e. Rhodes, Delos, Cyprus, the Black Sea coast[468].

146. Inv. no. 14/1988
Late Hellenistic House, in the loose soil on the stylobate of the portico
Dimensions: 4 × 1.7 cm

Νυσίου statue

Stamps of the producer Nysios are characterized by a representation of a statue on a base shown next to his name[469]. Grace dates him to the years 175—146 B.C.[470], a view corroborated by the concurrence of his stamps with those of the eponyms Pausanias III[471] and Anaxiboulos[472] among others.

Stamps of Nysios are not very widespread[473].

147. Inv. no. 18/1978
Surface find from the Villa of Theseus
Dimensions: 4 × 1.6 cm

Νυσίου statue

Stamp of Nysios, see above.

148. Inv. no. IP/1981
Surface find from the vicinity of the Villa of Theseus
Diam.: 3.2 cm

Νώλου head of Helios

There are no grounds for a more exact definition of the period of Nolos' activity, for no stamps of his have been recorded in well-dated assemblages or on amphorae preserving stamps of eponyms. On the basis of the token which recalls tokens from the second half of the 2nd cent. B.C., Šelov dates a stamp from Tanais accordingly[474].

[467] Bleckmann 1907, p. 31. The name of the eponym is partly destroyed and may be read either as the name of the eponym Aristeidas (see above, note 261) or as the name of Aristodamos. The latter is dated by Grace to the year 179 B.C., see Grace 1985, p. 8. See also Badal'janc, p. 165.

[468] Nilsson, no. 321; Grace 1952, p. 527; Calvet 1982, no. 69; Pridik, p. 31, nos. 754—761; Levi 1964, p. 271, nos. 294—295; Šelov 1975, p. 113, nos. 423—426; Lazarov 1977, p. 39, no. 84; Breccia, p. 40, no. 143; Sztetyłło 1983, p. 92, no. 67; Sztetyłło 1990, nos. 28—29; Reisner, p. 312; Macalister, p. 359; Crowfoot, p. 383; Gentili, p. 75, no. 142; Pellegrini, p. 241, nos. 339—340; Brugnone, p. 63, no. 95.

[469] Z. Sztetyłło, "Quelques problèmes relatifs à l'iconographie des timbres amphoriques. La représentation des statues", *ÉtTrav* III, 1966, pp. 46—80.

[470] Grace-Savvatianou, pp. 304—305, nos. E 10 and E 12.

[471] As above and Badal'janc, p. 165.

[472] Porro, nos. 47—48. See also Porro, nos. 3—4: combination Nysios — Aratophanes.

[473] Nilsson, no. 334; Paris 1914, p. 314, LXVI; Grace 1950, no. 56; Grace-Savvatianou, no. E 10; Šelov 1975, no. 436; Sztetyłło 1984, no. 12.; Säflund, no. 10; Crowfoot, p. 383; Breccia, p. 41; Gramatopol-Poenaru Bordea, Dacia XIII, nos. 732, 774, 1150.

[474] Šelov 1975, no. 437.

149. Inv. no. 16/1987

Late Hellenistic House, in upper layer of baulk between sectors 3/87 and 4/87

Dimensions: 4 × 1.7 cm

Rectangular stamp with one line of inscription and a torch represented to the right of the text.

Ὀλύμπου torch

Stamp of the producer Olympos with a token characteristic for him — a torch. Stamps of this producer have been found in Pergamon[475], Olbia[476], Tarsus[477] and Rhodes[478]. The Pergamon and Olbia finds supplied a certain dating placing him in the end of the 3rd and beginning of 2nd cent. B.C., while a combination with the eponym Ainesidamos II[479], in the form of concurring stamps, narrowed down the activity of Olympos to the years 210—175 B.C.[480]

150. Inv. no. 1/1976

Villa of Theseus, room 76, above mosaic floor level

Dimensions: 4 × 1.6 cm

Ὀλύμπου torch

Stamp of Olympos. See above.

151. Inv. no. 12/1978

Villa of Theseus, well in room 69, layer 1

Dimensions: 4.1 × 1.7 cm

Ὀλύμπου torch

Stamp of Olympos. See above.

[475] Schuchhardt, no. 1160.
[476] Levi 1964, nos. 299—303, pl. XX.
[477] Grace 1950, pp. 136, 141, no. 31. See also Šelov 1975, no. 439.
[478] Nilsson, no. 343; Paris 1914, p. 314, LXXI.
[479] Pridik 1926, p. 329 and 331; Badal'janc, p. 165.
[480] Grace 1963, p. 328 note 1; Grace 1953, p. 122, no. 14; Grace 1952, p. 528; Grace 1950, no. 31; Sztetyłło 1984, no. 8; Sztetyłło 1976, nos. 16—19.

152. Inv. no. 10/1983
Villa of Theseus, sector 3/82/83 in the northern wing, upper layer
Dimensions: 4×1.5 cm
Rectangular stamp with one line of inscription and a herm on a base represented lying horizontally to the left below the text.
ʽΡόδωνος herm

The producer Rhodon II, whose stamp we have here, was one of the Rhodian producers who placed a representation of a herm next to his name[481]. A combination with the eponym Aristratos places him before the year 150 B.C.[482] Perhaps he continued being active in the second half of the 2nd cent. B.C., for there is some similarity between the stamps of Rhodon and those of the producer Kallon who also used a representation of a herm on his stamps and who is dated to the second half of the 2nd cent. B.C.[483]

Stamps of Rhodon are not among the more common Rhodian stamps[484].

153. Inv. no. 23/1986
House of Aion, room 1, on top of a layer of ashes ca 1.36—1.40 m down from the surface
Dimensions: 4×1 cm
A long rectangular stamp with one line of inscription and a representation of a torch to the right of the text.
Σωκράτευς torch

Stamps of the producer Sokrates were recorded in Pergamon[485] and Villanova[486] among others. This gave a general dating to the end of the 3rd and beginning of 2nd cent. B.C. An analysis of the names of eponyms concurring with that of Sokrates allowed Grace to place him between 212 and 185 B.C.[487] Among the eponyms there were officials from the end of period II as well as from the beginning of period III. They included Xenophanes II[488], Hieron I[489], Archidamos[492], Sostratos[492] and Symmachos[493].

[481] Z. Sztetyłło, "Les hermes dans l'iconographie des timbres amphoriques grecs", *EtTrav* V, 1971, pp. 92—103
[482] Nicolaou-Empereur, pp. 523—524, no. 8.
[483] Šelov 1975, pp. 116—117, nos. 447—448.
[484] Grace 1934, nos. 61—62; Nilsson, no. 369; Pridik, p. 32, no. 821; Lazarov 1977, p. 40, no. 100; Šelov 1975, pp. 116—117, nos. 447—448; Breccia, p. 43; Crowfoot, p. 384.
[485] Schuchhardt, nos. 1188—1190.
[486] Maiuri, p. 262.
[487] Grace-Savvatianou, p. 302, no. E 3; Grace, Kyme 1, pp. 94—95.
[488] Schuchhardt, p. 426; Grace 1934, p. 219; Bleckmann 1907, p. 22 and 31; Badal'janc, p. 165.
[489] See above and Grace, Kyme 1, p. 95.
[490] Grace 1934, p. 219; Badal'janc, p. 165; Bleckmann 1907, p. 22 and 31; Reisner, p. 311.
[491] Grace, Kyme 1, p. 95, A 4; Grace 1974, p. 199; Badal'janc, p. 165; Levi, Iasos, p. 548.
[492] Grace-Savvatianou, p. 302, no. E 3, p. 303, no. E 5; Badal'janc, p. 165.
[493] Grace-Savvatianou, p. 371; Grace, Kyme 1, p. 96, A 4.

Stamps of Sokrates with the torch — a characteristic token of his — were common in the ancient world[494].

154. Inv. no. 1/1987
Late Hellenistic House, sector 1/87, south of room 48B of the Villa of Theseus, upper layer
Dimensions: 4 × 1.7 cm
Rectangular stamp with one line of inscription and a representation of a torch to the right of the legend.
Σωκράτευς torch

Stamp of the producer Sokrates. See above.

155. Inv. no. 19/1977
Surface find from the Villa of Theseus
Dimensions: 4 × 1.3 cm
Σωκράτευς torch

Stamp of Sokrates. See above.

156. Inv. no. IP/1981
Surface find from the vicinity of the Villa of Theseus
Dimensions: 3.2 × 1.5 cm
Τιμαράτου

Stamp of Timaratos considered to be a producer of period V on the basis of a combination with a stamp of eponym Thersandros[495]. His stamps are found very often[496].

[494] Nilsson, p. 382; Paris 1914, p. 315, LXXXII; Porro 1916, p. 120, no. 177; Maiuri, p. 262; Grace 1952, p. 528; Levi-Pugliese Caratelli, p. 615, no. 53; Levi, Iasos, p. 555, no. 29; I. Nicolaou, *RDAC* 1970, p. 162 no. 30; Calvet 1978, p. 227, no. 39; Calvet 1982, p. 13, nos. 87—88; Sztetyłło 1976, nos. 128—130; Grace 1934, p. 227, no. 48; Grace 1953, p. 119 note 7; Grace 1950, p. 141, no. 32; Pridik, p. 33, nos. 823—827; Levi 1964, p. 271, no. 314; Šelov 1975, nos. 452—454; Lazarov 1977, p. 40, no. 106; Gramatopol-Poenaru Bordea, Dacia XIII, p. 264, no. 1151; Canarache, p. 265, no. 649; Breccia, p. 44, no. 171; Reisner, p. 312; Dunand II, 2, p. 800; Macalister, p. 362; Börker, p. 35, no. 5; Empereur 1977, p. 227, nos. 81—82; Sztetyłło 1975, p. 186; nos. 95—96; Sztetyłło 1978, p. 280, nos. 35—36; Gentili, p. 85, no. 171; Pellegrini, p. 252, nos. 430—439; Brugnone, pp. 66—67, nos. 101—104.

[495] Sztetyłło 1976, no. 210 and no. 188. See also the activity of Thersandros: Brugnone, no. 18; Grace 1985, p. 13 note 24.

[496] Nilsson, no. 403; Grace 1952, p. 528; Šelov 1975, no. 464; Calvet 1982, no. 90; Sztetyłło 1990, no. 87; Crowfoot, p. 384; Breccia, p. 45.

157. Inv. no. 23/1976
Villa of Theseus, sector V/76, below the mosaic
Dimensions: 3.7 × 1.6 cm
Τιμαρχίδευς

There are no grounds to date the stamps of the producer Timarchides. His stamps are very rare.

See Nilsson, no. 404.

158. Inv. no. 1/1983
Villa of Theseus, sector 6/83, below the debris of wall N-S
Dimensions: 3.5 × 1 cm
Πανάμου
Φιλαινίου

Stamps of Philainios were recorded at Pergamon[497]. Concurring eponymical names narrow down the dating to 182—176 B.C.[498]

The stamps are encountered on numerous archaeological sites[499].

159. Inv. no. 7/1987
Late Hellenistic House, northern end of sector 1/87, at a depth of ca 1 m, below the debris of the eastern part of a longitudinal wall, south of room 48B of the Villa of Theseus
Dimensions: 3.9 × 1.4 cm
Rectangular stamp with a two-line inscription:
Πανάμου
Φιλαινίου

Stamp of the producer Philainios, month Panamos. See above.

[497] Schuchhardt, nos. 1207—1212.

[498] They include: Athanodotos, see Grace 1985, p. 10; Agestratos II, see Badal'janc, p. 165; Xenophanes II, see Bleckmann 1907, p. 22 and 32; Grace 1934, p. 219; Nilsson, p. 164; Grace 1968, p. 176, no. 9; Badal'janc, p. 165. Among the other eponyms one should mention Aristodamos, see Nicolaou-Empereur, p. 518, no. 4; Pratophanes, see Grace 1934, p. 219; Nilsson, p. 154; Maiuri, p. 266; Gentili, p. 28; Grace 1968, p. 176, no. 9; Badal'janc, p. 165. One should also mention Philodamos, see Bleckmann 1907, pp. 22—23; Grace 1934, p. 219; Badal'janc, p. 165, and Kratidas, see Porro, no. 108; Gentili, p. 28.

[499] Nilsson, no. 422; Paris 1914, p. 316, LXXXVIII—LXXXIX; Porro 1916, p. 122, no. 200; Grace 1952, p. 528; Calvet 1972, nos. 44—45; Calvet 1978, p. 227; Sztetyłło 1976, no. 136; Sztetyłło 1984, p. 368, no. 9; Grace 1950, p. 141, no. 33; Pridik, p. 33, nos. 848—854; Levi 1964, p. 272, nos. 320—321; Šelov 1975, no. 468; Lazarov 1974, p. 50, no. 90; Lazarov 1977, p. 41, no. 115; Breccia, p. 46, no. 191; Nachtergael, p. 44; Sztetyłło 1978, p. 280, nos. 37—38; Sztetyłło 1990, no. 34; Reisner, p. 312; Macalister, p. 362; Crowfoot, p. 384; Criscuolo, no. 129; Gentili, p. 89, no. 184; Pellegrini, p. 257, nos. 467—474; Brugnone, pp. 68—70, nos. 106—109.

160. Inv. no. IP 30/1983
Villa of Theseus, northern wing, sector 3/82/83, layer 3
Dimensions: 3.5 × 2 cm
Rectangular stamp with two lines of inscription:
'Επὶ 'Α[...
Πανάμ[ου

Juding by the title at the start of the inscription the stamp belonged to an eponym. The first letters of the second line are the beginning of the name of the month Panamos. This kind of stamp should be dated to period IV or V.

161. Inv. no. 17/1986
House of Aion, room 3, upper layer
Dimensions: 2 × 1.6 cm
Rectangular stamp with a two or three-line inscription, preserved fragmentarily:
....
....
]νθίου

The ending of the name of a month preserved in the last line belongs to either Hyakinthios or Sminthios.

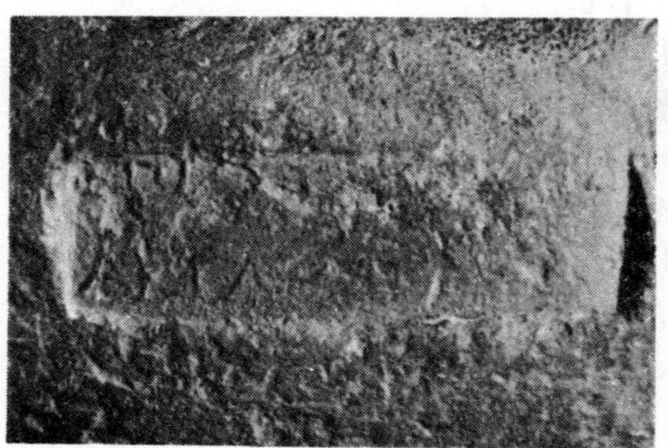

162. Inv. no. IP 17/1982
Surface find from the area of the Villa of Theseus
Dimensions: 3.8 × 1.6 cm
Rectangular stamp with two lines of inscription:
'Επὶ[
'Αρταμιτίου

The preserved title indicates this to be the stamp of an eponym; unfortunately, his name has been obliterated. In the second line there is the name of the month Artamitios.

163. Inv. no. IP 1982
Surface find from the Villa of Theseus
Dimensions: 4 × 1.5 cm
Rectangular stamp with two lines of inscription:
'Επὶ Αἰ[
['Υακι]νθίου(?)

The title at the beginning indicates this to be the stamp of an eponym, whose name has been obliterated. In the second line there is the name of the month, either Hyakinthios or Sminthios.

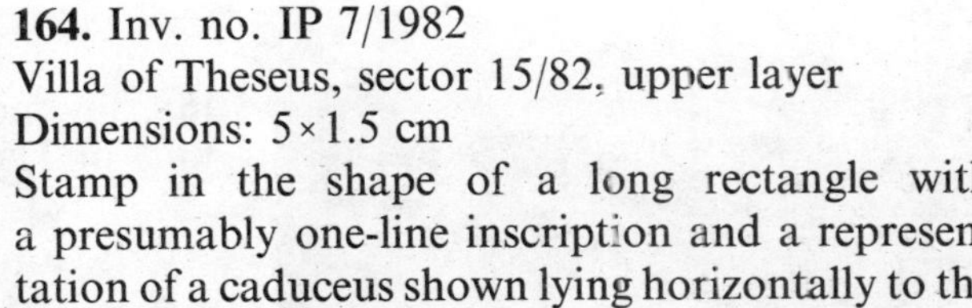

164. Inv. no. IP 7/1982
Villa of Theseus, sector 15/82, upper layer
Dimensions: 5 × 1.5 cm
Stamp in the shape of a long rectangle with a presumably one-line inscription and a representation of a caduceus shown lying horizontally to the right below the text.

]   caduceus

Judging by the shape of the stamp and the kind of representation this should be considered a stamp of a Rhodian producer of period IV or V. The caduceus is present especially often on the stamps of producers Eukleitos, Hieron and Midas; perhaps our stamp belongs to one of them.

165. Inv. no. IP 27/1983
From the Villa of Theseus
Dimensions: 4 × 1.2 cm
Stamp in the shape of a long rectangle, presumably with a one-line inscription. Below the text there is a representation of a caduceus lying horizontally to the right, while a bunch of grapes is shown to the right of the obliterated inscription.

]   caduceus and bunch of grapes

The stamp may belong to the producer Midas.

166. Inv. no. 37/1983
Villa of Theseus, sector 11/82/83, pit 1 (northeastern part of the villa)
Dimensions: 4 × 1.7 cm
Rectangular stamp with one line of inscription and a representation of a star or eight-leaf rosette.

]νος   star or rosette

Of the presumable producer's name only the ending in the nominative (?) has been preserved. The sigma is lunate, the type of stamp suggests a date in the 2nd cent. B.C.

167. Inv. no. IP 10/1982
Villa of Theseus, northwestern part of the residence
Dimensions: 3 × 1.6 cm
Part of a rectangular stamp preserving the end of a one-line text.

'Επὶ Δορ[
[Δα]λίου

A possible stamp of the eponym Dorchylidas. Cf. no. 40 above.

168. Inv. no. 7/1976
Villa of Theseus, sector I/76
]ν[
]ιου

Part of the name of a month preserved in the second line.

169. Inv. no. 7/1977
Surface find from the Villa of Theseus
[ ]
'Αρταμιτίου

The second line preserves the name of the month Artamitios.

170. Inv. no. IP/1979
From the vicinity of the Villa of Theseus
'Επὶ [
Θεσμοφορίου

The stamp of an eponym judging by the title. The name of the month Thesmophorios is preserved.

171. Inv. no. 8/1979
Villa of Theseus, room 86, upper layer
'Επὶ [
Π [ανάμου]

The stamp of an eponym. The name of the month Panamos is preserved.

172. Inv. no. 35/1978
Villa of Theseus, northern wing
'Επὶ [ ]
ν[ ]ας
Πανάμου

The stamp of an eponym. The name of the month Panamos preserved.

173. Inv. no. 41/1978
Villa of Theseus, northeastern part

]νι[
ʽΥακιν[θίου]

Part of the name of the month Hyakinthios preserved in the second line. Eponym Phainilas dated to the second half of the 2nd century B.C. and the early 1st century B.C.?

174. Inv. no. IP/1981
Surface find from the vicinity of the Villa of Theseus
ʼΕπὶ Κ[ ]
ʽΥακινθίου

Stamp of an eponym, name of month — Hyakinthios.

175. Inv. no. 15/1975
Villa of Theseus, southwestern part
ʼΕπὶ [
]νου[
ʽΥακινθίου

Stamp of eponym, the month's name — Hyakinthios.

176. Inv. no. 33/1987/IP
Villa of Theseus
Dimensions: 3.5 × 1.5 cm
Rectangular stamp with two lines of an obliterated inscription:

....
[Δα]λί [ου]

The end part of the name of the month Dalios has been preserved in the second line.

177—187. Inv. nos. 4/1975, IP/1981, 43/1978
Fourteen rectangular stamps with obliterated surfaces.

INDETERMINATE CIRCULAR STAMPS

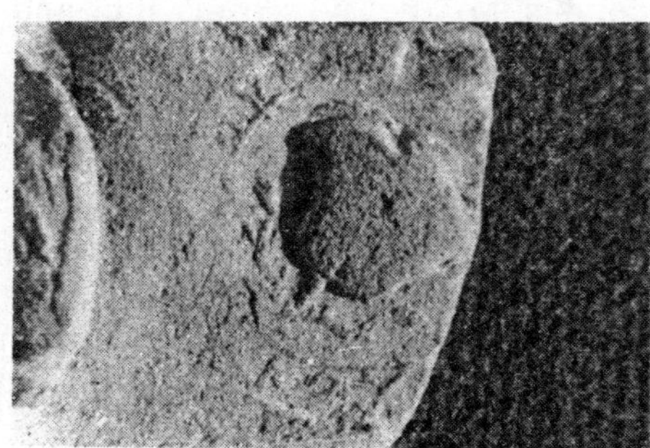

188. Inv. no. IP/1986
Villa of Theseus, southern wing, sector 1 B/W/86, above wall with preserved mural
Diam.: 3 cm
Circular stamp with a representation of a rose and preserved ending of a name:

]κου rose

This may be the stamp of the producer Andronikos dated to the second half of the 2nd cent. B.C. He used both rectangular and circular stamps[500].

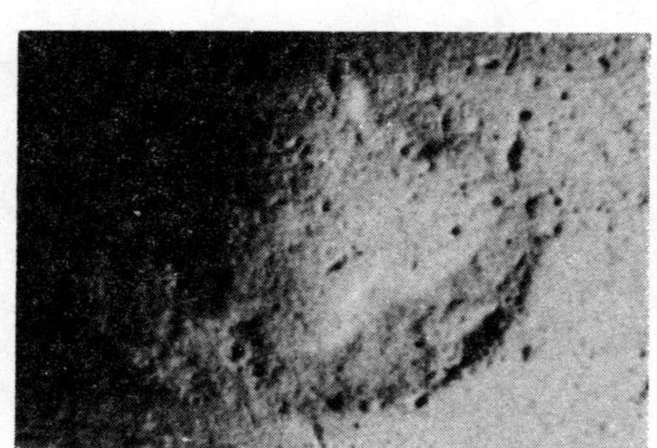

189. Inv. no. 6/1986
Late Hellenistic House, sector 1 B/W/86, upper layer
Diam.: 3 cm
Part of a circular stamp with a representation of a rose and some letters.

Δα]λίου rose

Presumably the end of the name of a month.

190. Inv. no. IP 37/1983
Villa of Theseus
Diam.: 3 cm
Circular stamp with obliterated surface, but preserving a representation of the head of Helios in the centre.

]ι[head of Helios

This type of representation is especially common in the second half of the 2nd cent. B.C.

[500] Nilsson, no. 50. In the period before 150 B.C. there was also an eponym called Androneikos, see Sztetyło 1976, no. 142.

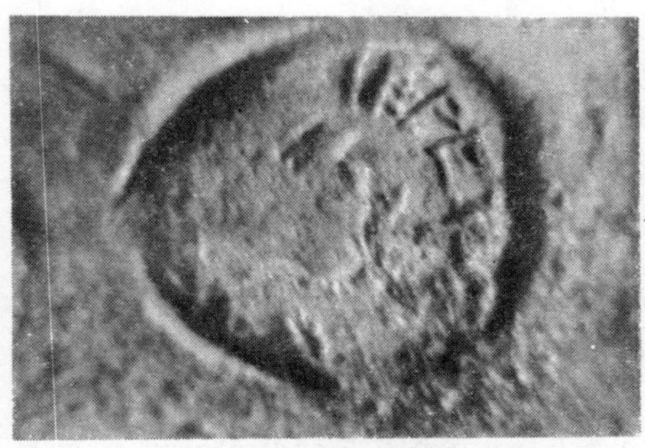

191. Inv. no. 14/1976
Villa of Theseus, sector III/76
'Επὶ ἱερέως [rose
Stamp of an eponym preserving the titles.

192. Inv. no. 42/1978
Villa of Theseus, northeastern part
] Σμινθίου rose
Only the name of the month Sminthios has been preserved.

193—211. Inv. nos. IP/1979, IP/1981, IP/1982—1987 and nos. 32/1978, 44/1978, 33/1980, 13/1982, 18/1982, 19/1982, 9/1982, 14/1982. Circular stamps with images of a rose (19 examples), surface obliterated.

STAMPS ON LAGYNOI

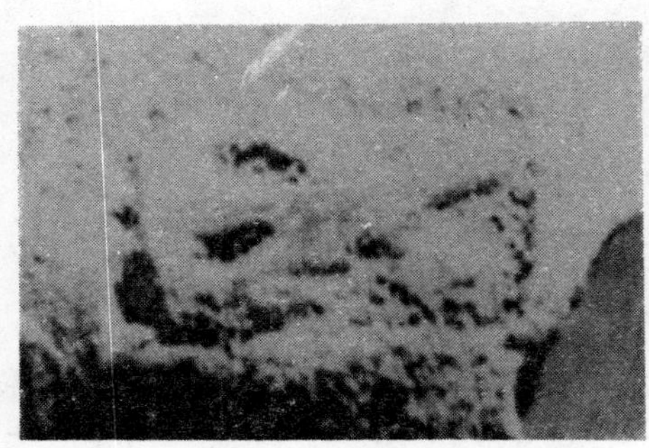

212. Inv. no. 24/1977
Villa of Theseus, western part, room 80, upper layer
EX (reversed?)
This kind of monogram and stamp are very close to the abbreviation of the month Hyakinthios on the stamps of the eponym Echeboulos, who is dated by Grace to the end of the 2nd and beginning of 1st cent. B.C.[501]

213. Inv. no. IP/1981
Villa of Theseus, in baulk between sectors III and IV/81
ΜΒ
The closest analogies are from the Pnyx and are dated to the end of the 3rd and beginning of the 2nd cent. B.C.[502]

[501] Grace-Savvatianou, no. E 43; Sztetyłło 1984, p. 313, pl. LXX, 2.
[502] See Grace 1956, no. 203; Grace 1952, p. 519, pl. XXV, nos. 37—38; Sztetyłło 1984, p. 313, pl. LXX, 1.

CHIOS

214. Inv. no. 9/1987
Late Hellenistic House, southwestern part of sector 4/87, in the debris of regular blocks from the house destroyed by a quake
Dimensions: 2.5 × 1 cm
Long rectangular stamp with one line of inscription:
Ἱκεσίου

One of the most frequently encountered names on stamps from Chios. Stamps of Hikesios were recorded on the Athenian Agora[503], the Pnyx[504] and also in Cyprus[505]. Grace dates Hikesios to the middle of the 3rd cent. B.C.[506]

215. Inv. no. 13/1977
Villa of Theseus, northwestern part
Ἱκεσίου

Stamp of Hikesios. See above.

NIKANDROS GROUP

216. Inv. no. 17/1984
House of Aion, sector 18—19/1984, layer above mosaic floor
Dimensions: 5 × 0.7 cm
A long oblong stamp. The tall letters of the one line of inscription fill the space entirely.
Μηνοφίλου

The name of Menophilos is mentioned by Marcadé among the stamps discovered on Delos[507]. An abbreviated form of this name appears also on a stamp published by Grace-Savvatianou[509]. Stamps from the so-called Group of Nikandros are dated rather generally to the Hellenistic period and their provenance is as yet unknown[509].

[503] Grace 1934, nos. 240—241.
[504] Grace 1956, no. 198.
[505] Sztetyłło 1976, nos. 360—362. See also Sztetyłło 1983, no. 351.
[506] See notes 292—293 above.
[507] J. Marcadé, "Terasse des Dieux Etrangers, Chronique des fouilles en 1953", *BCH* LXXVIII, 1954, pp. 217—220.
[508] Grace-Savvatianou, p. 367, no. E 245, contains the information that stamps of Menophilos were found in Athens, Alexandria and Corinth.
[509] Grace-Savvatianou, pp. 365—366.

217. Inv. no. IP/1981
Surface find from the vicinity of the House of Dionysos
'Απολλ (ωνίου)

Stamp of Apollonios or Apollonidas. Hellenistic period.

218. Inv. no. 28/1978
Villa of Theseus, northern wing, upper layer
'Ατύς

Stamp of Atys. Hellenistic period.

219. Inv. no. IP/1981
Surface find from the vicinity of the Villa of Theseus
Κοτε[ῦς](?)

Stamp of Kotes(?). Hellenistic period.

220. Inv. no. 14/1977
Villa of Theseus, from nearby the mosaic of Achilles, upper layer
Κύρου

Stamp of Kyros. Hellenistic period.

221. Inv. no. 6/1984
Villa of Theseus, northern wing, sector 2/82/83, eastern end, upper layer
Dimensions: 4.1 × 0.9 cm
The stamp is placed on one section of a double-barrel handle; it is a long rectangular stamp with one line of inscription and a horizontally placed club to the right represented below it.

]αμπίτου club

The name is that of Lampitos or Dampitos. The stamp is probably Hellenistic.

CNIDUS

222. Inv. no. 8/1977
Villa of Theseus, northwestern part of the residence
'Αρίσται-
ν(ος) 'Ε[ρατίδας]

Stamp of the *duoviri* Aristainos and Eratidas, dated by Grace to 97—88 B.C.[510]

223. Inv. no. 26/1971
Villa of Theseus, room 80, upper layer
'Επὶ Θεύδοτ[ου]
]πολ[

Grace places the activity of Theudotos in the period 188—187 B.C.[511]

224. Inv. no. IP/1981
Found in the vicinity of the Villa of Theseus
'Επὶ 'Ιεροκλεῦς
'Αγαθοκλῆς
Κνιδίον

The eponym Hierokles was active, according to Grace, in the second half of the 2nd century B.C., before the year 110 B.C.[512]

[510] Grace-Savvatianou, E 11, E 164; Grace 1985, p. 35 and p. 31.
[511] Grace-Savvatianou, no. E 51; Grace 1985, p. 33; Lenger I, no. 9, pl. XXIII.
[512] Grace-Savvatianou, nos. E 72, E 77 and E 64 as well as E 193. See also Grace 1956, no. 145, and Grace 1985, p. 33 and 37.

225. Inv. no. 25/1977
Villa of Theseus, room 80, upper layer

]ι[
Κρά[της]

Quite probably a *duoviri* stamp. Only the bottom line is preserved with the name of Krates, thus from the period ca 107—98 B.C.[513]

226. Inv. no. 32/1986
Villa of Theseus, southern wing, sector 1/1986, above the floor of a Hellenistic-Roman room
Diam.: 3.2 cm
Part of a circular stamp with a representation of a bucranium in the centre and the ending of an encircling inscription preserved.

]κράτου 'Αρισ[bucranium

Possibly the stamp of *duoviri*, 2nd-1st cent. B.C.

227. Inv. no. 10/1982
Surface find from the Villa of Theseus
Dimensions: 5 × 1.6 cm
Rectangular stamp with two lines of inscription, the beginning of each preserved.

'Επὶ[
[Κν]ιδίον

The name of the eponym is largely obliterated, while the bottom line contains the *ethnicon*, 2nd-1st cent. B.C.

228. Inv. no. 23/1982/P
Found in the Villa of Theseus
Dimensions: 3.4 × 1.5 cm
Rectangular stamp with two lines of an obliterated inscription.

[513] Grace-Savvatianou, nos. E 82, E 117 and E 168, and Grace 1985, p. 35.

229. Inv. no. 11/1982
Found in the Villa of Theseus
Part of a rectangular stamp with two lines(?) of an inscription; reversed(?)
αρ[

UNIDENTIFIED STAMPS

230. Inv. no. 4/1985
Villa of Theseus, western wing, sector 2/85, upper layer

Clay is similar to Rhodian clays, the handle slightly flattened, oval in section.
Dimensions: 2.6 × 1.8 cm
'Αρχοκ-
κράτη ⟨ς⟩

The name of Archokrates preceded by titles is known from Rhodian stamps[514]. The activity of this eponym has been dated to period III in view of the presence of his stamps in Pergamon and other well-dated archaeological contexts of the end of the 3rd and beginning of the 2nd cent. B.C.[515] In period V there was an eponym Archokrates who co-operated with the producer Drakontidas, that is assuming his stamp has been read correctly[516]. There was also an Archokrates Archipolios who was active before the so-called "Pergamene" period, fulfilling various priestly functions around 231 B.C.[517] Possibly this is a stamp of this eponym. It may also be the stamp of an unknown producer from the middle of the 3rd cent. B.C., for it recalls the stamp of Demetrios and the eponym Aretakles found on a Rhodian amphora dated by Grace to about 240 B.C.[518] It cannot be excluded, however, that this is a stamp from the so-called Parmeniskos Group, even though the name of Archokrates has not yet been recorded in it[519].

[514] Nilsson, no. 137.
[515] Schuchhardt, nos. 967—977. For a discussion of the stamps of the eponym Archokrates see Nachtergael, pp. 39—40, no. 13.
[516] Nachtergael, p. 40 note 6.
[517] Brugnone, p. 31, no. 12 and note 83, connects a stamp from Lilibeo with the activity of this eponym.
[518] Grace 1986, p. 559, figs. 5, 27, 28, and p. 564, no. 23.
[519] Grace 1956, p. 168.

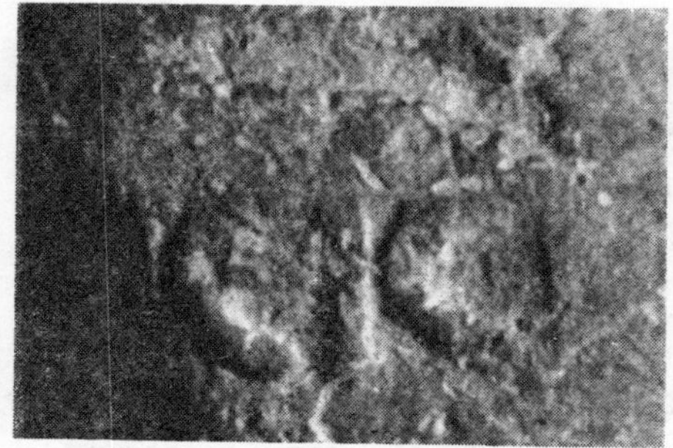

231. Inv. no. 1982/P
Villa of Theseus, northern wing, upper layer
Fine creamish clay, no visible impurities. Handle slightly flattened, oval in section.
Dimensions: 2 × 1.5 cm
Part of a rectangular stamp in an engraved frame. One-line inscription, *epsilon* and *sigma* rounded.
[Μαν]έις

Analogous stamps of Manes were found in Alexandria, but their provenance and dating are unclear as yet[520].

232. Inv. no. 4/1981
Villa of Theseus, sector I/81, in ceramic deposit
ΧΙΤΩИΙΦ

Reversed stamp(?). The clay type, shape of the handle and of the stamp itself recall stamps from Chios. See Sztetyłło 1988, p. 313, pl. LXX, 3.

233. Inv. no. 34/1979
Villa of Theseus, sector IV
Φήμμ-
ων

Handle oval in section. Reddish clay with creamy surface, no visible impurities. Rectangular stamp with large letters.

234. Inv. no. IP/1979
Found nearby the Villa of Theseus
E

Handle slightly flattened, oval in section. Reddish clay with a red surface, sand grit.

[520] A stamp from the Polish excavations on Kôm el-Dikka in Alexandria, inv. no. 684/1982, and Breccia, p. 51. For the name of Manes see also Grace-Savvatianou, p. 358; Grace 1956, p. 175, no. 255; Grace 1963, p. 320 and 321 note 1; Nilsson, p. 99.

235. Inv. no. 10/1984
House of Aion, room 1, southern sounding
Creamish-beige clay with a buff surface. Handle slightly flattened, oval in section.
Dimensions: 2.5 × 0.8 cm

Oval stamp with a representation of an amphora with an oval body narrowing down into a cylindrical foot, a long neck and small arched handles.

It would appear that this is a stamp belonging to a Corinthian amphora of type B, which may be dated to the second quarter of the 3rd cent. B.C.[521]

LATIN STAMPS

236. Inv. no. 1/1985/P
Villa of Theseus, northern wing, sector 5/85, upper layer

Amphora rim of light buff clay. The clay of the rim and its shape, not to mention the shape of the stamp itself, are close to that of rims with the stamps of T. Helvius Basil[522].
Dimensions: 4 × 1.7 cm
Stamp in sunk relief.
CT

Possibly CTARI or CTESII, Italic?[523].

237. Inv. no. 12/1977
Villa of Theseus, eastern part
CTYC
Stamp on a handle which is massive, almost round in section, of a light yellowish clay.
2nd cent. A.D.[524]

[521] C.C. Koehler "Amphoras on Amphoras", *Hesperia* 51, 3, 1982, pp. 284—289. The closest analogies are nos. 12 and 16 on pp. 288—289, pl. 78, see also p. 287. Calvet 1978, p. 230, no. 71, publishes an example of an oval stamp with a representation of an amphora, stating that it is a stamp of unknown provenance. See op. cit., p. 228, fig. 2.
[522] See cat. nos. 242—243.
[523] Callender, nos. 487—488.
[524] Callender, no. 494.

238. Inv. no. 31/1986

Villa of Theseus, southern wing, sector 1/86, upper layer

Light yellowish clay, double-barrel handle preserving stamp.

Dimensions: 5.5 × 1.2 cm

Long rectangular stamp with one line of reversed inscription:

[DION] ISIO ALBI [NI]

The fragment of stamp preserved has been theoretically reconstructed as DIONISIO ALBINI. Callender publishes stamps with the abbreviations ALB., ALBINI, ALBINH, which have analogies is the material from Monte Testaccio and which are dated to the reign of Antoninus Pius[525]. In Callender's opinion amphorae with this kind of stamp should be considered of southern Spanish origin[526].

If in the case of the stamp from Paphos the name in question is that of Dionysios, it is to be found in the Monte Testaccio material. The stamp's origins are also determined as southern Spanish (like the ALBINI stamps) and the date of their production is set around 154 B.C.[527]

239. Inv. no. 5/1987

Villa of Theseus, western wing, sector 10/87, upper layer

Part of the rim of a bowl with long rectangular stamp, the letters large and convex, forming one line of text.

ITALI

Stamps with the name ITALI are related to the colony founded in Spain by Scipio. Beside some rare exceptions, stamps of this type come from Monte Testaccio where they are dated to the period before the end of the reign of Antoninus Pius (138—161 A.D.)[528].

[525] Callender, p. 67, nos. 60—61.

[526] Callender, p. 67, nos. 62—63.

[527] Callender, p. 122, no. 545 and nos. 542—544. See also C. Lamour — F. Mavet, "Glanes amphoriques. II. Regions de Montpellier, Sete, Enserune, Le Cayle (Mailhac)", *Études sur Pezenas et l'Herault, Bulletin trimestriel édité par Les Amis de Pezenas* XII, 1981, 3, p. 11, no. 22.

[528] Callender, p. 157, no. 870. See also no. 186.

240. Inv. no. 8/1983
House of Aion, room 1 (northeastern corner), upper layer

Pinkish-buff clay, porous with grit of medium size. Preserved section of a stamped bowl rim.
Dimensions: 5×2.7 cm
One-line inscription in raised relief, large letters filling the field of the rectangular stamp.
L. LENT.

Callender thought some analogous stamps to be Italic and dated them to ca 50 B.C.[529]

241. Inv. no. 23/1977
Villa of Theseus, eastern part of the "tower", upper layer
L. Q

Stamps L.Q.A., L.Q.I., L.Q.R. and L.Q.S. are related to the southern regions of Spain and are dated to A.D. 80—130[530]

242. Inv. no. 10/1984/P
Villa of Theseus, east of sector 8/1978, upper layer
Double-barrel handle of light yellowish clay. A single letter on one of the barrels, without any frame or band.
M

This kind of stamp has a few analogies including a stamp from Mt. Beuvray dated to the year 5 A.D. Single letters on Roman amphorae are also encountered earlier[531]. The piece from Mt. Beuvray is thought to be of Italic origin[532].

243. Inv. no. 23/1977
Found near the Villa of Theseus
METROBIUS (BETILIENI)

An import from Spain, 2nd cent. A.D.[533]

[529] Callender, no. 881; Sztetyłło 1984, p. 313.
[530] Callender, nos. 910—922; Mayet 1978, no. 44, pl. VII; Lamour, p. 5, no. 3, and index nos. 94—95, pl. V; Sztetyłło 1978, no. 107.
[531] Callender, no. 993.
[532] As above.
[533] Callender, no. 192 c and no. 1079; Sztetyłło 1976, no. 392; Le Roy, BIFAO 84, p. 313, no. 34.

244. Inv. no. 6/1978
Villa of Theseus, southeastern part
T.P.C.
Fragment of a stamp on the neck of an amphora; it has analogies in the 2nd cent. A.D.[534]

245. Inv. no. 30/1986
South of the southwestern corner of the Villa of Theseus, sector 1/86, above the floor of a Hellenistic-Roman room
Clay reddish-beige with medium size grit. Stamp impressed on the rim of a large bowl.
Dimensions: 5.5 × 3.5 cm
Rectangular stamp with two lines of inscription in high relief, finely formed letters. The two lines separated by an ornamental vegetal scroll.
SGENTI
LIAYG

A similar bowl rim fragment with a two-line inscription separated by an ornamental design was found in Paphos in the 1969 field season[535]. The form of the stamp would suggest a date in the period at the turn of the 1st cent. B.C. and 1st cent. A.D.[536]

246—247. Inv. nos. 19/1984 and 2/1985
The stamp 19/1984 was found in the northwestern corner of the Villa of Theseus, the other — 2/1985/P in the western wing of the villa, in room 23 (sector 2/85), layer 4
Both are fragments of the necks of a light-buff clay.
Dimensions: 3 × 2 cm and 4.5 × 1.7 cm
Stamps are in sunk relief:
T.H. [B].

The closest analogies are stamps from Castel Pretorio[537], from a deposit of amphorae dated to the 1st cent. B.C./1st cent. A.D.[538] Callender and Bohn consider them the stamps of the father of T. Helvius Basil, *legatus* during the reign of Claudius and Neron[539].

[534] See Callender, no. 1733; no. 234.
[535] See Sztetyłło 1976, p. 102, no. 386.
[536] Callender, p. 82, no. 186, fig. 4, 17.
[537] Dressel, "Di un avande deposito di anfore rinvenuta nel Nuovo Quartiere del Castel Pretorio", *Bulletino Comunale* VII, 1879, nos. 30, 17, 32.
[538] As above.

248. Inv. no. 29/1983
House of Aion, room 3, above mosaic floor level
Dimensions: 6.5 × 2.5 cm
Rectangular stamp with two lines of inscription in high relief:
ALEXAN
DRILADA

Hayes considers the ALEXANDRILADA stamps to be rare Latin stamps belonging to the group of stamped North Syrian mortaria which are quite widespread[540].

249. Inv. no. 16/1985
Villa of Theseus, western wing, room 21, upper layer
Dimensions: 5.4 × 2.8 cm
Rectangular stamp with two lines of inscription in sunk relief:
Διονεί-
κου

The name of Dioneikos is common among the names on stamps encountered on Syrian mortaria. As in the majority of the cases of stamps of this group, Hayes considers the 3rd cent. A.D. as the date of their origin[541].

250. Inv. no. 40/1986
Villa of Theseus, western wing, room 21
Mortarium rim with eleven stamps of Dioneikos.
Dimensions: 5 × 2.7 cm
Rectangular stamp, double impressed line of text.
Διονεί-
κου

See above.

[539] Callender, p. 258, no. 1717.
[540] Hayes, pp. 340, 339, no. 98, pl. 3, pp. 342—346; Sztetyłło 1984, p. 313.
[541] Hayes, loc. cit.; I. Nicolaou, *RDAC* 1968, p. 79.

251. Inv. no. 1/1982
Villa of Theseus, northern wing, upper layer in sector 1/82
Dimensions: 5.1 × 2.6 cm
Rectangular stamp with a double line of inscription, impressed, within a relief frame.
Διοφάν-
του βου( )

Beside those of Dioneikos, the stamps of Diophantes are the most common mortarium stamps[542].

252. Inv. no. 9/1976
Villa of Theseus, sector III/76
Διοφάν-
του β( )

Stamp of Diophantes. See above.

253. Inv. no. 5/1979
Villa of Theseus, southern portico no. 25
Δόμ-
νου

Stamps of Domnos have been found in Nea Paphos before and are dated like the other mortarium stamps[543]. See above.

254. Inv. no. 2/1983/P
Villa of Theseus, northern wing, sector 10/83, room 53, upper layer
Dimensions: 2.8 × 2 cm
Part of a rectangular stamp with two lines of inscription in high relief in a relief frame:
'Ερμογ-
ένουσι

Stamps of Hermogenes were recorded in Attica, Egypt, Syria, Palestine and in other regions[544].

[542] Hayes, loc. cit.
[543] Sztetyłło 1976, nos. 384—385. See also Sztetyłło 1978, nos. 102—104; Hayes, pp. 342—346.
[544] Hayes, loc. cit.

255. Inv. no. 8/1984 (IP 7/1984)
Villa of Theseus, northern wing, sector 12/83/84, layer 2
Dimensions: 7×4 cm
Part of a rectangular stamp with a double line inscription in high relief, set in a relief frame. A horizontal relief line separates the two lines of inscription.

Mε[

.....

The upper line is partly obliterated, the bottom line has been destroyed. There are no grounds for identification or dating.

INDEXES

The numerals in boldface refer to catalogue entries, the other are page and note numbers

I. NAMES OF PERSONS

a) Greek names

Mutilated

b) Latin stamps

II. RHODIAN MONTHS

III. TITLES

IV. ETHNICS

V. ATTRIBUTES AND MONOGRAMS